THE BOOK OF THE DEAD

THE BOOK
OF THE DEAD

Papyri of Ani, Hunefer, Anhaï

Commentaries by
Evelyn Rossiter

LIBER

THE EGYPTIAN BOOK OF THE DEAD
REU NU PERT EM HRU, OR THE CHAPTERS OF COMING FORTH BY DAY.

The Egyptian Book of the Dead is a loose collection of invocations and magic spells, usually written on papyrus rolls with illustrations, which, from about 1600 BC onwards, were placed in the tombs of those Egyptians who could afford them. Their purpose was to enable the deceased to overcome the dangers of life after death, mainly by making it possible for them to turn into any of a number of powerful creatures, by teaching them passwords for the various stages of the Underworld, and by securing for them the protection of the gods, while at the same time proclaiming their identity with many of those gods.

What the Book of the Dead is *not*

Since the real nature of the Book of the Dead has often been misunderstood, we might as well begin by saying clearly what it is not.

First of all, it is not a book of ritual. Virtually the entire text is spoken, or intended to be spoken, by the deceased himself, and not by a priest. It is true that some chapters have elements of ritual in them, but these are exceptions of no significance.

The Book of the Dead is not really a book: the title by which it was known to the ancient Egyptians was *Reu nu pert em hru,* or "Chapters of coming forth by day". The name "book", which suggests a composition with some kind of unity, one written at a certain time by a certain author or authors, was given to it by the German scholar Richard Lepsius. In 1842 Lepsius published the great Turin Papyrus under the title *Das Todtenbuch.* After that the name stuck, and has been used by Egyptologists ever since.

It is also a mistake to think of the Book of the Dead as a kind of ancient Egyptian Bible or sacred scriptures. In the solemn, archaic style so appropriately used by Budge, Renouf and others in their translations of this work, some parts of the Book of the Dead do remind us of the very moving grandeur of the Hebrew Psalms; indeed the Jewish holy books were influenced to some extent by the religious writings of Egypt; but the resemblance ends there.

Although the Book of the Dead does give us an insight into Egyptian religion and funerary beliefs,

it is not a body of dogma or revelation for the guidance of the faithful. Quite apart from anything else there is no single papyrus which contains all the 190 separate independent chapters of the whole collection. In an attempt to form a standard collection of these chapters, the priests of Thebes and Saïs did establish what are now known as the Theban and Saïte Recensions; however, these are not really "authorized versions" as we understand the term.

In fact, even the word "chapters", applied to the work by the scribes of the 12th dynasty (c. 1800 BC), is also misleading, as it suggests unity and coherence. "Spells" or "magic formulas" would be more accurate.

Lastly the Egyptian Book of the Dead is in no way similar to the work known as the Tibetan Book of the Dead, *Bardo Thödol.* In this Buddhist work, the whole of human experience, before and after death, is viewed as a vast, persistent illusion. The Egyptians, on the other hand, were in no doubt at all as to the reality of their world. Their religious beliefs, as portrayed for example in the Book of the Dead, seem to us fantastic and at times incomprehensible. Yet the Egyptians were an intensely practical, down-to-earth people, not given to indulging in abstract metaphysical thinking.

Fantasy and conservatism

This dislike for abstract theorizing, coupled with the innate conservatism of the ancient Egyptians, is responsible for one of the most striking features of their religion: its extreme complexity. The Egyptians were reluctant to abandon old ideas, gods and myths, even while adopting new ones. Instead, they tried, somehow, to reconcile and harmonize them, thus making their theology more and more complex with the passage of time.

"Theology", of course, may not be a suitable term, as it implies a carefully thought out and consistent pattern of ideas and divine relationships. At various times the priests of each of the main cult centers, at Heliopolis, Memphis, Thebes and Hermopolis did attempt to put their respective beliefs into some kind of order. But one can hardly say that there was ever a truly unified and nationwide theology in Egypt.

The selections from the Book of the Dead contained in the Papyri of Ani, Hunefer and Anhai certainly reflect some of the confusion that resulted from such attitudes. The tone of the monologue which takes up most of the text fluctuates wildly from boasting to humble entreaty to threats against the gods and back to abject servility, all on the same page in some instances. The deceased identifies himself with the great god of the dead, the dead king Osiris, calling himself "Osiris-Ani", etc. Yet, despite such immensely powerful protection, he continues to seek magic ways of combating the dangers of the Underworld, and invoke the protection of lesser gods.

What happened to the dead in the next life was also a confusing and confused subject. They might go to the Fields of Peace, rise into the sky to live as stars, be united with Osiris in his dominion over the Underworld, ride with Re in his solar barque, or, apparently, do any combination of those things.

A most notable inconsistency occurs in Chapter 125, the Protestation of Innocence. Here the deceased assures forty two gods that he has done no wrong in his lifetime, listing all the sins he has not committed. On the one hand this chapter suggests that the Egyptians had a strong sense of morality, while on the other it is plain that they expected the words themselves to win their acquittal by magical means.

Magic and religion

Egyptian religion laid great stress on the formal cult of the gods, and, until a very late period, very little on personal piety. Indeed the Egyptians had no word for "religion" as we know it. The word *hike,* which means roughly the "magic power of words", comes closest to reflecting the substance of their religion and the beliefs underlying the Book of the Dead. Unlike our modern clergy, Egyptian priests were devoted almost exclusively to the details of the cult and were not involved in the spiritual welfare of the ordinary people. In any case, these latter were not allowed to enter the sacred inner sanctuaries where the shrines of the deities were located; their main religious acts were the great religious festivals, such as the spring festival of Osiris, symbolizing rebirth, and certain popular religious practices.

Not that magic was confined to religion—it permeated the whole of Egyptian life. Magic spells were often recited while drugs were being administered to the sick; and oracles could be consulted to resolve disputes over property. Numerous papyri have survived which contain collections of spells against disease and other adversity, such as the Harris Magical Papyrus and the Calendars of Lucky and Unlucky Days. Amulets inscribed with magic symbols such as the Knot of Isis, the Eye of Horus and the *djed* column, as well as spells invoking divine protection were commonly placed in tombs.

An optimistic book

One distinctive feature of the samples of funerary literature we are considering here, and of Egyptian religion in general, is their very positive attitude to life after death. Our three papyri tell us about what awaits those whose heart, when weighed against the feather of *maat,* or truth, is found satisfactory: they can expect to go to live in the Fields of Peace, ride with Re in his solar barque, etc. But we are told nothing at all about hell. In the scene of the Weighing of the Heart it is not even made clear whether the heart of the deceased is supposed to weigh more or less than the symbolic feather in the other pan of the scales. And the monster Ammit, the "Eater of the Dead", seems to do little actual devouring: he simply sits by the scales, next to the scribe-god Thoth, waiting. Egypt had no Hieronymus Bosch to paint the torments of the damned and the horrors of hell. Throughout the Book of the Dead the deceased is identified with Osiris, being called "Osiris-Ani triumphant", etc., and apparently feels assured of the support and intercession of many other gods. The question of failing to achieve eternal bliss simply does not arise.

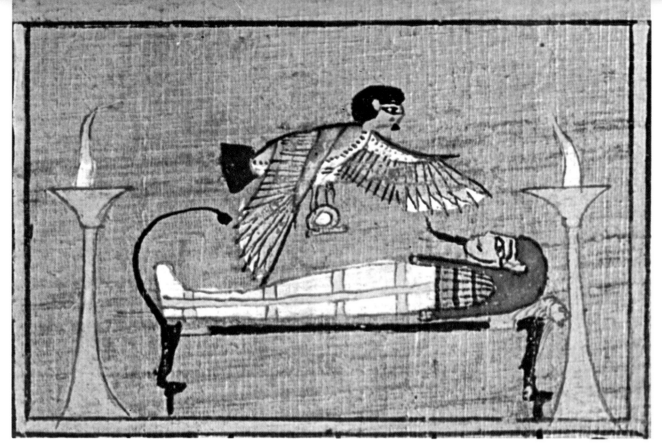

A very positive fascination with death

There is no doubt that the inhabitants of the Nile valley had believed in life after death long before the foundation of ancient Egypt in about 3100 BC. Of course, they were not alone in this among the peoples of the ancient world. However, the idea that the extreme dryness of their climate has much to do with the emphasis they laid on the preservation of the body is not very convincing: other nations lived in similar climates in ancient times, but none had the advanced funerary beliefs of the Egyptians.

What distinguished them was the extraordinary lengths to which they went in expressing their beliefs about life after death. Ornate mummies and coffins were quite expensive, while the burials of kings and nobles must have consumed whole fortunes. After all, the spectacular tomb of Tutankhamun, which had already been partly looted by the robbers of antiquity before Howard Carter reached it in 1922, belonged to a young and fairly minor king. The contents of the tombs of the great pharaohs must have been literally fantastic.

Why were the ancient Egyptians so concerned with death? A modern reader, with rational Western habits of mind, could be excused for doubting the sanity of a people which buried such immense wealth and beauty and allowed the thought of death to dominate its cultural and political life to such an extent.

One would expect to find a nation of morose, dejected people, brooding over inevitable calamity, or seeking an escape from unbearable living conditions. In fact quite the opposite is true. The ancient Egyptians feared death precisely because of all they had to lose. Unique among the ancient, and even among many more recent civilizations, they lived in a rich land blessed by nature with abundant resources, a fertile valley watered generously by a great river; moreover, they had more than their fair share of kings who, though despots, were inspired by ideals of responsible government. For much of their history they enjoyed the kind of peace which can alone be provided by geographical isolation—the barriers of the Western Desert, the sea and the Sinai Peninsula.

From kings to commoners

As democratic ideas gained ground in Egyptian society, so the funerary texts also changed in character: they became available to far more people, and were increasingly influenced by the cult of Osiris at the expense of the aristocratic sun-god Re. Originally, in the form of the Pyramid Texts, they had been intended to provide help in the after-life only for the semi-divine kings, who were thought to have special magical powers in common with the gods. Then, after the collapse of strong central authority between 2250 and 2050 BC (the First Intermediate Period), they took the form of the Coffin Texts. Lastly came the much more democratic—and *cheaper*—Book of the Dead.

The pyramid is the main symbol of the sun-god;

and the pharaohs who built the lavish structures near the site of modern Cairo were certainly fervent worshipers of the sun-god Re, whose cult was based at nearby Heliopolis. On the whole they were distinctly hostile to the new and revolutionary cult of Osiris; some pyramids contain strongly worded inscriptions to that effect.

The pyramid of Unas, built about 2345 BC, was the first in which the walls and vestibules of the burial chamber were covered with religious texts dealing with the king's welfare after death. This example was followed by other Old Kingdom pharaohs. The Pyramid Texts, not unlike the Book of the Dead a thousand years later, contained magic spells, prayers, hymns, myths and some ritual.

Next came the Coffin Texts. The spells and other formulas once reserved for the king could now be used by nobles and high officials who, finding pyramids well beyond their means—and, in any case, no longer in fashion—inscribed the funerary texts on their coffins.

From the beginning of the New Kingdom, about 1580 BC onwards, after the turmoil of the **Second Intermediate Period**, the funerary texts came to be written on papyrus rolls. Salvation now came more nearly within the reach of the common man. Papyrus, though cheaper than pyramids and coffins, still cost money however; and Ani, **Hunefer** and Anhai were rich people. Yet, as Budge observes, there was no reason why a man should not write his own papyrus, or use the services of an ordinary scribe to produce a shorter selection of chapters from the Book of the Dead, or one with fewer or less brilliant illustrations.

The sacred city of Thebes

Thebes, where our three papyri were produced and, some three thousand years later, discovered, was one of the most famous cities of the ancient world. Its rise to greatness began shortly after 2000 BC, when the local nomarchs, or governors, united Egypt under their rule. Some 450 years later they greatly consolidated their fame and power by driving out the Hyksos, invaders. The prosperity and power of Thebes reached a pinnacle during the New Kingdom (c. 1580-1150 BC), when the pharaohs, enriched by booty from Asia and tribute from Nubia, sought to outdo their predecessors in magnificence of construction. The Papyri of Ani and Hunefer, therefore, coincide with the heyday of Theban prosperity; by the time the Papyrus of Anhai was produced, about 1100 BC, a decline had begun. Thebes was shaken by scandal in high places, economic difficulties and a series of incidents in which royal mummies were plundered in their burial-places.

The local god of Thebes, Amun, provides perhaps the best example of a phenomenon which occurred frequently in Egyptian religion: formerly obscure gods could be projected to national fame as a result of the temporal power of the area in which their cult center was based. Amun became assimilated with the old state sun-god Re, and was known as Amun-Re. The wealth which was amassed by the priests and temples of this god far surpassed that of the rival centers Memphis and Heliopolis. A papyrus written during the reign of Ramses III (1198-1166 BC) shows that Thebes had nearly ten times more head of livestock and seven times more personnel than Heliopolis; it had 65 hamlets, 46 workshops, 83 boats and 433 gardens.

The political and financial power of Thebes was matched by the predominance of its clergy in religious matters. Amun-Re became the great god of the Empire, and the High Priest of Amun assumed a sort of papal power, rivaling that of the secular rulers of Egypt. It was against this background that these three extraordinary documents were created.

Custom-made, or bought from stock?

Papyri bearing texts and vignettes from the Book of the Dead were items of merchandise like any other. The number and choice of chapters, the quality of the vignettes and the length of the papyrus all depended on the needs and the financial standing of the buyer. The great Turin Papyrus is 185 feet long. Good illustrated papyri of the Theban Recension (about 1580-1000 BC) are between 15 and 90 feet long, and 12 and 18 inches wide. By Graeco-Roman times, however, the

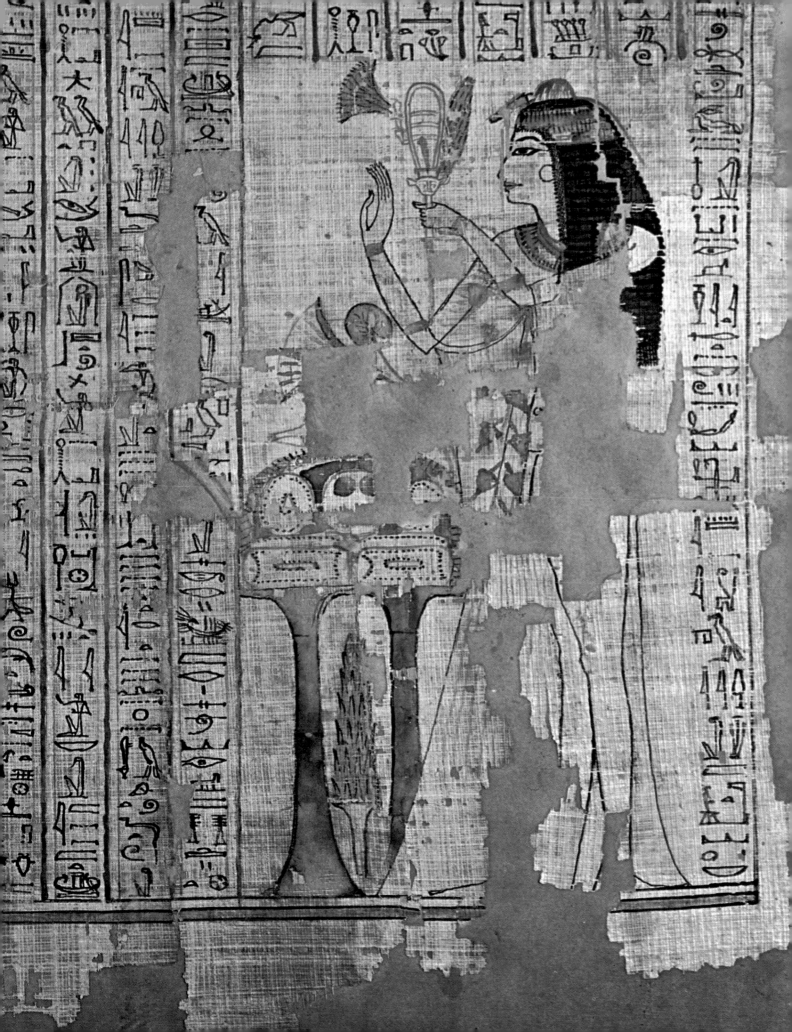

Book of the Dead scrolls were down to mere scraps of papyrus, some of them only a few inches square.

Papyri of the Book of the Dead were sometimes made specially to order for individual clients, according to their instructions; in other cases copies were bought from stock, and the name of the beneficiary was filled in later. This is thought to be the case in the second part of the Papyrus of Ani.

Originally the layout was decided by the scribe, the artist, if any, being required to fill in the blanks with illustrations. Gradually the papyrus came to be made in the reverse order: first came the vignettes, which predominate, for example, in all three of the papyri in this book, and then the scribe filled in the remaining columns, trying not to leave unsightly blank spaces, or find himself obliged to write in the margins.

Very often the vignettes are the work of a fine artist, while the texts—many of which contain errors, repetitions and unofficial additions made by the scribes themselves—are very carelessly done. In the Papyrus of Ani, for example, Chapter 18 is repeated.

The scribes, in any case, were not learned men. They sometimes failed to understand the ancient texts they were copying, reading them in the wrong direction, or deleting or omitting passages as they saw fit, for reasons of layout or personal taste.

The hieroglyphic script

All three of the papyri in this book are written in the hieroglyphic script; this was a distinctively Egyptian form of writing which, like so much else in that long-lived civilization, remained basically unchanged for over three thousand years.

The Egyptians used three types of script at different times and for different purposes. The word "hieroglyph" derives from a Greek term meaning "sacred carvings". It was widely used on monuments and in sacred texts throughout Egyptian history. The other two scripts were *hieratic and demotic*. Hieratic—from the Greek for "priestly", since the Greeks found it being used particularly by the priests—was a more flowing form of hieroglyphic, influenced by the flexibility of the reed pen rather than the rigidity of the chisel.

It was used from the earliest stages of Egyptian civilization, for religious, literary, business and official writing. Demotic—from the Greek word for "popular"—was a cursive form which developed from hieratic about 600 years before the birth of Christ, and was used mainly for secular purposes.

Hieroglyphic writing was extremely cumbersome; unlike other systems, it did not become easier or simpler with the passage of time. If anything, as the priests devised more and more ingenious signs and symbols, it became more complex. The script used pictures, signs and symbols to represent single, double and triple consonants, while certain hieroglyphs were added at the end of words to help illustrate their meaning.

Only consonants were represented, so we have to guess at the sound of most Egyptian vowels. Coptic, which derived from the language of ancient Egypt, is some help in identifying some of the vowel sounds. On the whole, however, a conventional *e* is placed between the consonants for the sake of convenience in modern transliterations.

The Papyri of Ani, Hunefer and Anhai

All three papyri were prepared for Theban dignitaries. Ani was a royal scribe, an accountant of the divine revenues of the gods, the manager of the granaries of the lords of Abydos and scribe of the lords of Thebes. His wife Thuthu was a "lady of the house and *qemat* of Amun-Re" at Thebes; she was therefore one of the noble ladies who acted as priestesses in the divine service, singing and playing musical instruments, including the sistrum which she is seen carrying throughout the papyrus.

Hunefer was an overseer of the royal palace of Seti I, king of Egypt about 1370 BC. His functions also included those of superintendent of the royal cattle and royal scribe. Like Thuthu, his wife Nasha was a member of the famous priesthood of Amun-Re at Thebes; she, too, is seen carrying a sistrum as she accompanies her husband in the vignettes.

Anhai was a singer in the college of Amun-Re. She is portrayed as being taller than the other two ladies in this book; like them she carries a sistrum and flowers, but the garment she is wearing seems to be completely transparent.

At slightly more than 78 feet, the Papyrus of Ani is the longest papyrus of the Book of the Dead from the Theban period; the Papyrus of Hunefer measures 18 feet 1 inch, and that of Anhai 14 feet 6 inches. With the exception of the first 16 feet or so, the Papyrus of Ani is thought to have been bought ready-made from stock, the name of the client being filled in later. Both the other two papyri seem to have been made specially for Anhai and Hunefer.

Many papyri were lost as a result of the manner of Anhai and Hunefer were protected from accidental damage by being placed inside a hollow part of a statuette of the triple deity Ptah-Seker-Osiris, representing the gods of Creation, Death and the Underworld. Fortunately for modern students of ancient Egypt this was a fairly common method of depositing the funerary text known as the Book of the Dead during the New Kingdom.

Nothing is known of the precise manner in which the papyrus of Ani was deposited in the tomb. This large papyrus was, however, in an excellent state of preservation when unrolled. All three papyri were bought from egyptian dealers by the trustees of the British Museum—the papyrus of Hunefer in 1852, and those of Ani and Anhai in 1888.

About this book

In this book we have reproduced, in th eir original order, all the vignettes from the papyri of Ani, Hunefer and Anhai. The length of the texts of the three papyri makes it impossible for us to include them in a publication of this sort. Instead, we have tried to convey something of the context in which these illustrations occur, by giving the title of the chapter or chapters to which each vignette is related and describing briefly the mood and substance of the texts. In addition, a number of extracts from the more important or interesting chapters are reproduced on separate pages.

Pictorial Glossary

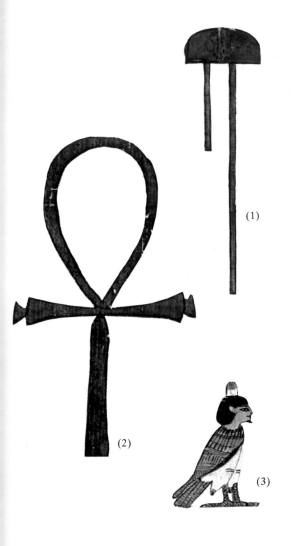

(1)

(2)

(3)

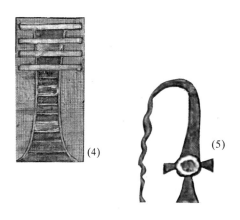

(4)

(5)

(6)

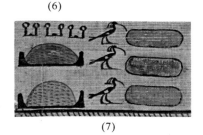

(7)

SYMBOLS

AMENTA

The Underworld. Originally the place where the sun set, this name was later applied to the West Bank of the Nile where tombs were hewn out of the rock. (1)

ANKH

The ansate cross, symbolic of life. (2)

BA

This spiritual entity is quite close to what we understand by the term "soul". The *ba* left the body at the moment of death. It was thought to spend the day assuming various forms in which it could be useful to the deceased, and at night it returned to the tomb. (3)

DJED COLUMN

The name of this extremely important symbol, which was particularly associated with Osiris, came from a word meaning "stable" or "durable". It was probably a pre-historic fetish based on the shape of a tree with lopped off branches, a stake with notches or a bundle of cut stems. The *djed* signified ascent or continued life. It was a common architectural and decorative motif and moreover played an important part in the Osirian rites during which it was ceremoniously erected. It is sometimes shown with eyes, and also with arms and the symbols of power. (4)

FLAME

This symbol, which is the same as the hieroglyphic sign for flame, depicts a brazier with smoke rising from it. (5)

KA

This is an elusive concept which was not understood in the same way by the Egyptians themselves at the various periods of their history. Generally speaking it means one's double, a kind of abstract entity which survived the death of the body; its principal abode was the tomb, which was in fact known as "the house of the *ka*", and it was for the *ka* that offerings of food and drink were left in the tomb. The arms in the symbol are usually regarded as being raised; Clark, however, considers that they are outstretched in the form of an embrace, and that they thus signify "to impart vital essence", that is, the power of the gods.

KHU

A spiritual entity often mentioned in association with the *ba*. It was viewed as an entirely spiritual and absolutely immortal being. (6)

MAAT

The concept of order, truth, regularity and justice which was all important to the ancient Egyptians. It was the duty of the

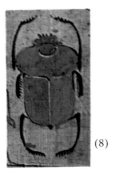

(8)

(9)

(10)

(11)

pharaohs to uphold *maat*. Both Osiris and Re are seen sitting or standing on the hieroglyphic sign in the papyri of Ani and Hunefer. (7)

SCARAB

The dung-rolling beetle was, to the ancient Egyptians, a symbol of regeneration and spontaneous creation, as it seemed to emerge from nowhere; in fact it came from eggs previously laid in the sand. Seals and amulets in scarab form were very common and were thought to possess magic powers. (8)

UDJAT

This important symbol is named after the "sound eye" of Horus. According to one version of the legend Seth, the god of evil intentions, snatched away the eye of Horus which then fell to pieces. Thoth found it and put it together again. The *udjat* was regarded as a powerful protective amulet; it is frequently found in tombs, on coffins and on the seal which was placed over the incision in the mummy through which the internal organs were removed. (9)

GODS

ANUBIS

The jackal-god of the necropolis, patron of embalmers and protector of mummies. It was Anubis who prepared the mummy of Osiris.

HATHOR (MEHURT)

A goddess with many functions: ruler of the sky, living soul of trees, nurse of the kings of Egypt, goddess of music, dancing and love. The head of Hathor—a woman's face with a cow's ears— was used as a motif on temple columns and sistrums. Mehurt, in the form of a cow, was identified with Hathor. (10)

HORUS

A number of Egyptian gods had this name, the earliest of them being a sky-god whose emblem was a falcon. Here we are dealing with Horus the Younger, son of Isis and the dead Osiris, who avenged his father's death by defeating his brother Seth and winning the support of the other gods. As the opponent of Seth he was regarded as the patron and protector of the king. The ruling pharaoh was entitled "The living Horus", as his incarnation on earth. His cult-centers were at Hierakonpolis and Edfu, in Upper Egypt, and also at Behdet in the Delta. (11)

THE FOUR CHILDREN OF HORUS

The gods of the four cardinal points, the "sovereign princes of Osiris". From the left: Hapi, Mestha, Tuamutef, Qebhsennuf. These minor deities were assigned the role of protecting the internal organs after they had been removed during mummification and placed in Canopic jars. In fact, the stoppers of these jars were made in the likeness of each of these gods.

ISIS

Both wife and sister of Osiris; mother of Horus the Younger. Usually shown in a protective role.

KHEPERA

The beetle-headed god often identified with Re; associated with the idea of creation.

MAAT

Goddess of truth, order, regularity and justice. Although she was thought of, in some versions of the divine world, as the daughter of Re and the wife of Thoth, and although she had her own temple at Karnak, Maat stood slightly apart from the rest of the gods. The notion which she embodied was usually thought of in more abstract terms, as the concept *maat* rather than the deity Maat. (12)

MEHURT

The divine cow, another form of Hathor.

NEPHTHYS

The sister of Isis; also a protective goddess.

NUT

Sky-goddess, wife of the earth-god Geb.

OSIRIS

God of the Underworld, of the Nile flood and of vegetation, judge of the dead. Osiris was thought of as a dead king, a former ruler of Egypt, who, having been treacherously murdered by his jealous brother Seth, was miraculously brought back to life. Accordingly, he came to symbolize man's hope for life after death. The identification of the dead with Osiris, though originally a prerogative of kings and nobles, soon spread throughout Egyptian society. It was a result of the trend towards greater democracy and, at the same time, greatly influenced that trend. In our three papyri Osiris is often shown with a protective female escort, Isis and Nephthys. Whereas Re inspired in the ordinary people respect for overwhelming power such as that of the Egyptian sun, Osiris evoked both respect and compassion. He had suffered, died and yet was once more alive. He is often shown, for example, wearing the white bandages which were used on mummies. Osiris was worshiped throughout Egypt; his main cult center was at Abydos. (13)

RE

The great sun-god of Heliopolis. Re's position of eminence —like that of so many other members of the Egyptian pantheon—was partly due to geo-political factors. Heliopolis was not far from Memphis, where the kings of united Egypt first established their capital city. As the political unity of Egypt grew so did the importance of Re, while he was also a powerful unifying factor in a country which, on account of its extraordinarily long and narrow shape, did not readily

(15)

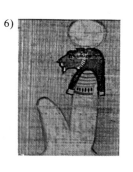

6)

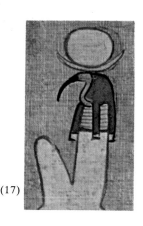

(17)

(18)

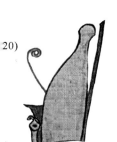

20)

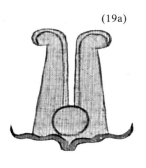

(19a)

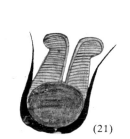

(19b)

(21)

lend itself to unification. About 2500 BC, during the 5th dynasty, the king came to be known as "the son of Re". A legend came into being to the effect that the sun-god had once been a ruler of Egypt. However, by the end of the New Kingdom (c.1150 BC), Re, who had long been associated in the popular mind with royal power and aristocratic prerogatives, had begun to lose favor, being replaced as judge of the dead by Osiris. (14)

SACRED APES

These apes were regarded as the Spirits of the Dawn, who were thought to turn into apes as soon as the sun had risen.

SHU

The god of air. (15)

TEFNUT

The goddess of moisture. (16)

THOTH

The scribe of the gods, source of all learning and science, master of the magic arts, moon-god. (17)

MISCELLANEOUS

BENNU BIRD

The Phœnix. Understood at various times as being a form of the primeval god, the patron of the reckoning of time, the soul of Osiris, the carrier of eternal light from the abode of the gods to the world of men, and the principle of life. (18)

ATEF CROWN (TWO VERSIONS)

The exact significance of this crown is not known, but it is thought to have been associated with universal power and dominion. (19a, 19b)

THE DOUBLE CROWN

A combination of the White Crown and the Red Crown of Lower Egypt. The Red Crown was worn by the kings of Lower Egypt, whose capital was at Buto, in the Nile Delta. The cobra is the emblem of Lower Egypt, Edjo, here symbolically protecting the king. This crown symbolized the union of Upper and Lower Egypt, which was achieved when the invaders from Hierakonpolis, under a semi-legendary king named Menes, conquered the Delta, in about 3100 BC. This event marked the beginning of the civilization which we know as ancient Egypt. (20)

QUEEN'S CROWN

Associated with Hathor. (21)

WHITE CROWN

This was the crown worn by the kings of Upper Egypt, whose capital was at Hierakonpolis, in the Late Predynastic Period, (c. 3300-3100 BC).

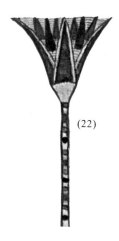

LOTUS

A symbol of birth and dawn; it was thought to have been the cradle of the sun on the first morning of creation, rising from the primeval waters. The lotus was a common architectural motif, particularly used on capitals. (22)

MENAT

A protective amulet invoking the divine favor. It was usually worn on a string of beads at the back of the neck, probably as a counterpoise to items of jewelry worn in front. Many of these amulets have been found in tombs. They were supposed to bring fertility to women and virility to men.

PYLON

A massive rectangular stone gateway at the entrance to Egyptian temples, leading to the open courts and pillared hyspostyle halls beyond which lay the enclosed sanctuaries of the gods. Pylons were hollow inside; they sometimes had staircases, and the bigger ones even had rooms. The two stone towers were thought to resemble the symbol for the horizon; it was for this reason that the king used to make his appearance on the roof between them, as the embodiment of the sun-god Re. (23)

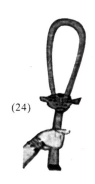

SISTRUM

The sistrum was a sacred noise-making instrument used in the cult of Hathor and other gods. The type illustrated in the Papyri of Ani, Hunefer and Anhai, known as the *iba,* was shaped like a closed horse-shoe. Another kind had the shape of a temple, and was known as the *seseshet.* The sistrum consisted of a wooden or metal frame fitted with loose strips of metal and mobile disks which made a jingling noise when moved. These instruments, which were thought to attract the attention of the gods, were carried to the temple by women of high rank, among them Thuthu, Anhai and Nasha, who appear in this book. (24)

Ushabti FIGURES

These statuettes were placed in the tomb with the mummy. They were supposed to have the power of sparing the deceased any hard manual labor in the Underworld. Since it was assumed that there would be work to be done, particularly after the annual Nile flood, these figures were to answer the call to work on behalf of the deceased. In some tombs of the late New Kingdom whole gangs of *ushabti* workers were included, including foremen carrying whips.

Was SCEPTER, FLAIL AND CROOK

The sacred *was* scepter, which occurs frequently in this book, was based originally on a shepherd's staff. The ancient name of Thebes, capital of Egypt in the New Kingdom, derives from the name of this scepter. The flail and crook represented power and dominion. (25)

The Papyrus
of Ani (c. 1420 B.C.)

1

"Hymn to Re at his rising". Ani and his wife
Thuthu worshiping the rising sun. Ani's hands are
raised in the conventional posture of adoration;
his wife holds in her right hand a Hathor-headed
sistrum and, in her left, a necklace and *menat*. They
stand before a table of offerings consisting of meat,
cakes, wine, oil, fruit and flowers.

"Hymn to Osiris-Un-nefer, the great lord of Abydos". The title "Un-nefer" means: "he who is always happy". Beneath the vault of the sky the solar disk is supported by two arms emerging from the symbol of life, the *ankh,* which rests on the *djed* column. On either side are Isis and Nephthys kneeling in adoration on the solar mount.

"Hymn to Osiris Un-nefer" (conclusion). Ani and Thuthu, again in the characteristic pose of adoration. This vignette is the same as the one which occurs at the beginning of the papyrus, but is undamaged.

4

The weighing of the soul of Ani in the Hall of Double *Maat,* Ani's address to his soul and the sentence of acquittal, in which he is found to be *maa-cheru* ("triumphant" or "true of voice" has been used to render this term). In the lower vignette Ani and his wife enter the Hall of Double *Maat,* where Ani's heart—the organ regarded by the Egyptians as the seat of conscience and understanding—is weighed against the feather of *maat,* symbolic of order, regularity, truth and justice. Anubis, the custodian of the dead, checks the balance to make sure that it is working properly; on the right, Thoth, the scribe of the gods, records the verdict on his scribe's palette. Behind him stands the monster Ammit, "Devourer of the Dead", whose body consists of the head of a crocodile, the trunk of a lion and the hind quarters of a hippopotamus. Thoth is shown again as the baboon at the top of the scales.

Like the Papyrus of Hunefer, which was produced some fifty years later, the Papyrus of Ani has a second vignette included in this judgment scene: in the upper register are twelve of the major gods who sit in judgment, before a table of offerings; each of them holds the sacred *was* scepter.

5

The address of Horus to Osiris, announcing that Ani has been found virtuous, followed by the prayer of Ani. Horus, the son of Isis, leads Ani into the presence of Osiris. Ani, his wig now whitened, kneels in adoration. Osiris sits on a throne within a shrine in the form of funeral chest, with his usual protective escort, Isis and Nephthys. Before him stand the four Children of Horus on a lotus flower. Above the shrine is the head of a hawk, emblem of Sokaris, the mortuary god of Memphis, guarded by twelve cobras.

6

The Egyptian title, for this part of the work, *pert em hru,* meaning "coming forth by day", was based on the belief that the soul spent the first night after death traveling to the Underworld, where it arrived next morning. In this triumphant passage Ani proclaims his identity with various gods, at the same time invoking their helps so as to have total freedom of movement—including, at one point in the text, the ability to enjoy "cakes and ale"—in the Underworld. The vignettes show the procession to the tomb and the funeral cere- mony. Ani's mummy, in a funeral chest on a boat, is drawn along by oxen. Thuthu kneels at the side. Small figures of Isis and Nephthys stand at either end of the boat. The man in the panther skin is a priest burning incense and sprinkling water. Behind him come eight male mourners. On the far left servants bring up the rear carrying some of Ani's household objects, including his scribe's palette, all of which are to be deposited in the tomb. They tow along a small funeral chest decorated with the emblem of Isis. On top of the chest is Anubis, in the same pose as that of his statue found at the tomb of Tutankhamun.

7

Title: "Giving a mouth to Osiris-Ani". The text of this chapter opens with the modern-souding line. "I shine forth out ot the egg that is in the unseen world." The "egg" is the rising sun. The men with the yokes over their shoulders are carrying boxes of ointments, flowers, etc; next comes a party of paid—and apparently skilled—female mourners, with bare breasts and heads. In front of them is a group of offerings of herbs and fruits; the cow and calf, which are to be offered at the funeral feast are thought to symbol-ize the sky and the rising sun respectively. On the far right at the door of the tomb, Thuthu kneels, in tears, before her husband's mummy, which is held protectively by Anubis. Behind her are a table of offerings and three priests; one reads the funeral service from a papyrus, while the other two are about to use the instruments shaped like a ram-headed serpent and an adze to perform the important ceremony of "opening the mouth and eyes" of the mummy. This ceremony was thought to restore the dead body's ability to see, breathe, eat and drink. Behind them lie the objects they are about to use.

8

Here, whereby the deceased is enabled to leave and enter Amenta (the Underworld) at will and in whatever form he pleases. Clark describes this very important chapter of the Book of the Dead as one of the most popular religious texts in ancient Egypt. The picture of Ani sitting in a hall playing drafts is a reflection of the title of the chapter in the Papyrus of Ani. The two birds are the souls of Ani and Thuthu, standing on a pylon. Next to them is an altar with offerings and lotus flowers.

9

The two lions are symbolic of Yesterday and Today (i.e., Osiris and Re). Between them is the solar disk, beneath the vault of the sky.

10

The *Bennu* bird, or heron of Heliopolis, which was symbolic of rebirth, next to a table of offerings. In the text the deceased identifies himself with this bird.

11

The mummy of Osiris-Ani lying on a bier, guarded by Isis and Nephthys. Beneath are some everyday objects, including a scribe's palette, for burial.

12

The deceased here declares that he can recognize certain figures and objects, some of which are shown in the vignette. They are the Spirit of the Eternal Waters (holding the emblem of long life, and with his hand stretched out over a pool containing the Eye of Horus); the god called the Great Green Lake (his hands held out over lakes of natron and nitre, in which Osiris is supposed to have been purified on the day of his birth); the gates to the Underworld, *Restau;* the *udjat* over a pylon; the goddess Mehurt; the gods accompanying Re, who is in a tomb holding two *ankh* signs (they are the Children of Horus).

13

Here Ani successfully identifies a number of
spirits who, together with the four Children of
Horus, are appointed by Anubis (fourth from left)
to protect Osiris. Far right: the two bird-like souls
between the *djed* pillars are Re and Osiris who,
as the text says, "meet in Tattu". Tattu was the
ancient name for Busiris, one of the two main cult
centers of Osiris, the other being Abydos.

14

Ani identifies the Cat, symbolic of Re, next to the persea tree, who is in the act of slaying the serpent of darkness, Apophis. Then follows an invocation of the beetle-headed god Khepera, who is floating across the sky in his solar barque. The god is asked to protect Ani against his enemies because he has now been declared to be pure. The apes watching the boat and the Eye of Re are identified in the text with Isis and Nephthys.

15

Conclusion of this part: Osiris-Ani now identifies himself with the god Tem, seen here sitting inside the solar disk in the boat of the setting sun. The protection of the lion god Rehu is then invoked. The serpent coiled around the lotus flowers, with the flame symbol, is Uatchit, the Lady of Flame, who crushes the powers of darkness and the enemies of Re.

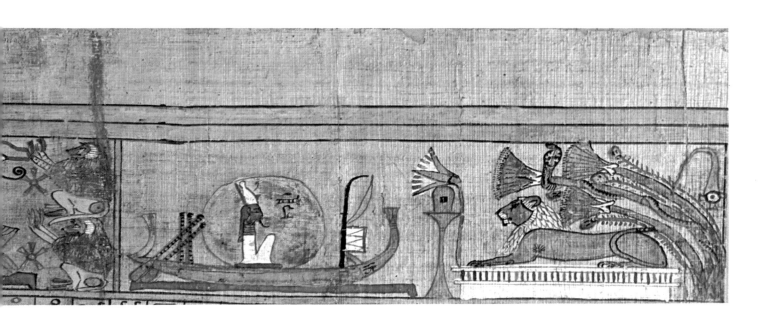

16

Texts concerning the Arits and the Pylons. The deceased is now required to memorize the names of the guardians of seven Arits, or mansions, and ten pylons in the Underworld. The Turin Papyrus has 15 such pylons, while some versions have as many as twenty. The spell contained in

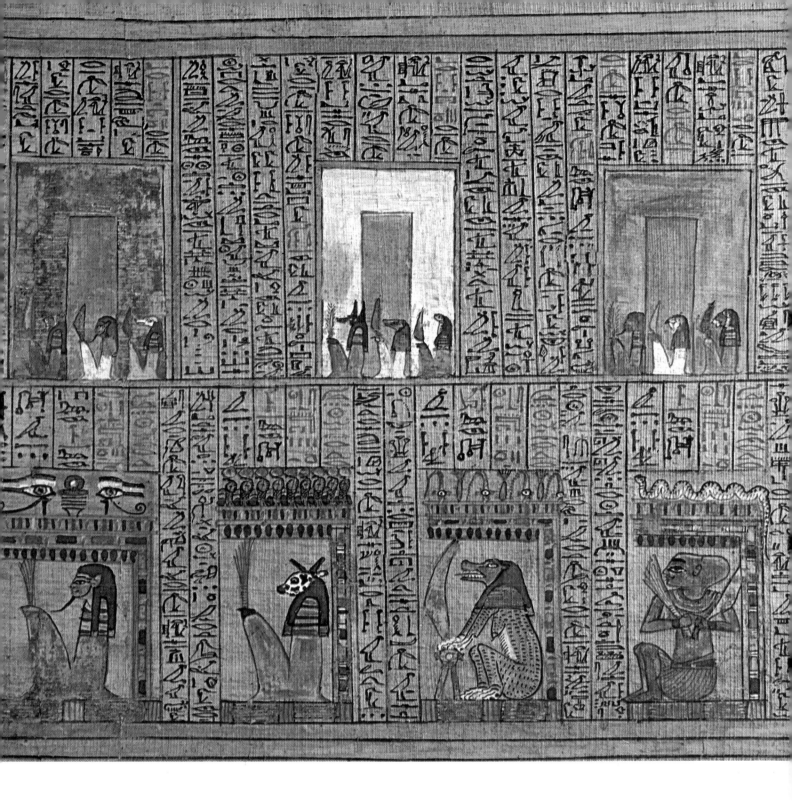

this chapter enables Ani to overcome each successive obstacle to eternal bliss. In the upper register, Ani and his wife Thuthu reverently approach the first Arit, the entrance to which is guarded by three gods, with the heads of a hare, a serpent and a dog. The second Arit is guarded by gods with the heads of a lion, a man and a dog. The third Arit is guarded by gods with the heads of a jackal, a dog and a serpent. In the lower register the couple approach the ten pylons. For some reason Thuthu is now holding her sistrum in her other hand. The now invincible Ani correctly names the first five doorkeepers and is thus allowed to proceed. Their names are Neri, Mer-Ptha, Ertat-Sebanque, Nekau, Henti and Requ.

17

The fourth Arit is guarded by gods with the heads of a man, a hawk and a lion. The fifth Arit is guarded by gods with the heads of a hawk, a man and a snake. The sixth Arit is guarded by gods having the heads of a jackal, a dog and a dog. The last Arit is guarded by gods having the heads of a hawk, a lion and a man. The names of the doorkeepers of the pylons (lower register) are Semani, Akenti, Khutchethf, Tchesef and Sekhem-Ur.

18

Invocations of the priests and Ani. Ani and his wife are introduced to the gods by the priests, who wear leopard skins and have the lock of hair characteristic of Harpocrates, god of youth.

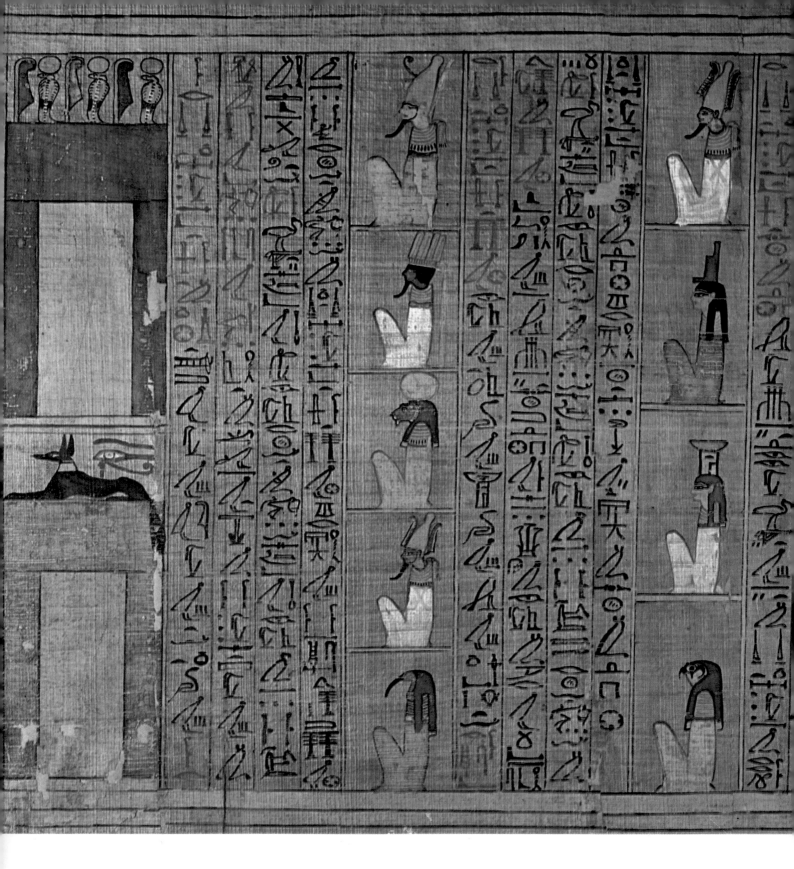

19

The Litany to Thoth, in which Ani is presented by the two priests to the gods of the main cities of Egyptian mythology. For Egyptians, evidently, the after-life consisted of a replica of the country and culture which they loved so dearly during their lifetime. Thoth is here asked to make Ani victorious, as he had once made. Osiris triumph over his enemies at those very places.

Place: Heliopolis Gods; Tem, Shu, Tefnut, Osiris, Thoth.
  Busiris   Osiris, Isis, Nephthys, Horus.
  Latopolis   Osiris, Horus, *two udjats* on pylon, Thoth.
  Buto   Horus, Isis, Mestha, Nephthys.
  Rekhti   Isis, Horus, Anubis, Mestha, Thoth.

20

The Litany to Thoth (conclusion).
Place: Abydos
        Place of judgment
        Tattu (Busiris)

Anrutf
Restau

Gods: Osiris, Isis, Anubis, *djed* column.
Thoth, Osiris, Anubis, Astennu.
The three festival gods of Tattu.

Re, Osiris, Shu, Bedi.
Horus, Osiris, Isis and an unnamed god.
Note that the scribe, evidently obliged to write
in his text after the vignettes had been completed,
ran out of space in the last column and had to write
on the border.

21

"Opening the mouth of the deceased". Ani implores Thoth, who is, *inter alia,* the supreme magician, to remove the bandages which cover his mouth. This was an important and ancient funeral ceremony considered vital to the dead person's chances of eternal happiness. Here we see a priest holding up the *ur-hekau,* a ramheaded snake-like instrument, about to touch the lips of the deceased. The text of which follows at this point in the Papyrus of Ani, has no vignette; in it the deceased asks to be given the magic formulas which will enable him to do as he wishes in the Underworld.

22   23

"Giving a heart to the deceased". The heart was important not only as a physical organ and as the seat of the conscience and under-standing, but also because it is thought to have been connected with the *ba* soul.

Holding his heart in his right hand Ani here addresses Anubis, the custodian of the dead. He holds strands of colored beads, the clasp of which bears the image of the sun-god Re-Harmakhis (= "horizon") in his solar barque. Ani's address to his heart, which follows chapter, has no vignette. The same text occurs in the Judgment Scene, and, for that reason, probably, has no vignette here.

"Not letting a man's heart be taken away from him". "Giving air". In the middle vignette Ani is holding an inflated sail, symbolic of air; in the outer two he is clutching a bird-shaped *ba* soul (left) and stands holding a staff.

24 to 30 (Above)

"Not letting a man's heart be taken away from him in the Underworld". Ani's heart is on a pedestal before four gods who are seated on the emblem of *maat*.

"Breathing the air and having power over the water in Amenta". Ani and his wife standing in water; they each hold an inflated sail, symbolizing air, in their left hand, and are scooping up water to drink with the right hand. Note the palm trees and clusters of dates—one of the numerous natural blessings of ancient Egypt.

"Breathing the air and having power over the water in Amenta". The skygoddess Nut, in the sycamore tree, gives Ani cakes and Water.

"Not dying a second time". An incantation against total extinction. Here Ani is seated before a table on which there are slices of bread.

"Not becoming corrupt in the Underworld". Ani's mummy is embraced protectively by Anubis.

"Not perishing and becoming alive in the Underworld". The *Bennu* bird and Ani's soul stand on either side of the door to the tomb.

"Not putting one's head on the execution block". Ani is seen standing with his back to an execution block and a bloodstained knife.

"Not letting a man's head be cut off in the Underworld". Ani adoring three gods, each of whom holds the *ankh* symbol and the *was* scepter.

"Not sailing to the east in the Underworld". Ani stands, his hands raised in adoration,

48

addressing god whose head is turned backwards to face him.

"Enabling the soul to be united with its body in the Underworld". Ani's soul, in the form of a hawk-headed bird, clutching the *shen*, emblem of eternity, in its talons, flies above the deceased mummy.

"Not letting the soul of Ani, triumphant, be made captive in the Underworld". Ani's soul, in the form of a human-headed bird, standing before a door.

31 to 33 (Below)

"Opening the tomb to the soul and shadow of Osiris". The bird-shaped soul and the shadow *(knaibit)* are seen to the right of the picture.

"Lifting up the feet and coming forth on the earth". The boat of Sokaris, the god of the necropolis, on its sledge.

"Passing through Amenta by day". Ani walks towards the Underworld.

"Coming forth by day after making the passage through the tomb". Ani stands in a pose of worship before a ram wearing the *Atef* crown and standing on a pylon; between them is an altar with a lotus flower and a libation vase.

"Enabling a man to come back to see his house on earth". Ani standing next to a house, a long staff in is hand.

"Against one's enemies". Ani slaying Apophis, the serpent of darkness.

34

Hymn to Re. The hawk-headed sun-god Re, seated in a boat floating on the sky. A tiny figure of the god Harpocrates is seated on the platform in the bows of the boat.

35

"Litany to Osiris". The great god of the dead is here invoked nine times, emphasis being laid each time on some different divine attribute of his. The responses are always the same; the deceased asks to be granted a path along which he may go in peace, as he is just, has not lied intentionally and has not acted deceitfully. Ani, with Thuthu, are here seen standing in the customary pose of worship.

36

"Litany to Osiris" (conclusion). Osiris, holding the traditional emblems of power and sacred authority, standing in a shrine with Isis.

37
Hymn of praise to Re. The hawk-headed sun-god Re, seated on the emblem of *maat,* floating across the sky in his boat; Ani is worshiping him.

38
"Making perfect the spirit". Re in his solar barque, facing an image of the starry sky.

39
"Making the spirit perfect". Like the preceding chapter, this is a psalm-like invocation of the wondrous powers of the sun-god for the benefit of Ani. Both chapters were also rituals to be performed by the relatives of the deceased on his behalf according to very precise instructions.

40

Litany to Thoth and presentation of Ani to the gods of the localities, is here repeated for some unknown reason.

41

"Going into the presence of the divine sovereign princes of Osiris". This spell was to be recited by the deceased on entering the presence of the chief ministers of Osiris, the four Children of Horus (of whom only three are shown here).

THE CHAPTERS OF TRANSFORMATIONS

42

The following eleven vignettes correspond to the chapters containing spells which were supposed to turn the deceased into certain powerful beings or to enable him to move freely throughout the Underworld, without being turned back.
"Transformation into a swallow".

Here the deceased makes a psalm-like invocation of the aid of the great gods.

I am Yesterday, To-day, and To-morrow, for I am born again and again; mine is the unseen Force, which createth the gods and giveth food to those in the Tuat at the West of Heaven; I am the Eastern Rudder, the Lord of Two Faces, who seeth by his own light; the Lord of Resurrections, who cometh forth from the dusk and whose birth is from the House of Death.

Ye two divine Hawks upon your gables, who are giving attentive heed to the matter; ye who accompany the bier to the tomb, and who conduct the ship of Re, advancing onwards from the highest place of the Ark in heaven—the Lord of the Shrine which standeth in the centre of the Earth;

He is I, and I am He.

Mine is the radiance in which Ptah floateth over his firmament.

Oh Re, who smileth cheerfully, and whose heart is delighted with the perfect order of this day as thou enterest into Heaven and comest forth in the East: the Ancients and those who are gone before acclaim thee.

Let thy paths be made pleasant for me; let thy ways be made wide for me to traverse the earth and the expanse of Heaven.

Shine thou upon me, oh gracious Power; as I draw nigh to the divine words which my ears shall hear in the Tuat; let no pollution of my mother be upon me; deliver me, protect me from him who closeth his eyes at twilight and bringeth to an end in darkness.

I am the Overflower, and Kam-ura is my name: I bring to its fulness the Force which is hidden within me.

Oh thou Great One, who art Shoreless, and callest upon the Powers of the South, at the moment when the god is carried forth, saying:—

"Behold the Lord of his Flood; see, the Shoulder is fastened upon his neck and the Haunch upon the head of the West" offerings which the two goddesses of the West present to me when the weeping bursteth forth from me at what I witness, as I am borne round on the Tenait in Abydos, and the bolts made fast on the gateways above your images are in the reach of thine hand and from within thee.

Thy face is as that of a hound whose nostril sniffeth at the covert to which my feet convey me.

Anubis is my bearer, for he who lulleth me to rest is the god in Lion form.

Do thou save me!

I am He who cometh forth as one who breaketh through the door; and everlasting is the Daylight which his will hath created.

In these brief passages, the deceased voices his fear of dismemberment and of total extinction (second death) and identifies himself with powerful sources of divine assistance.

I am a Prince, the son of a Prince; a Flame, the Son of a Flame, whose head is restored to him after it hath been cut off.

The head of Osiris is not taken from him, and my head shall not be taken from me.

I raise myself up, I renew myself, and I grow young again.

I am Osiris.

Let the Cavern of Putrata be opened for me, where the dead fall into the darkness but the Eye of Horus supporteth me, and Apuat reareth me up. I hide myself among you, O ye Stars that set not. My front is that of Re, my face is revealed, according to the words of Thoth; my heart is in its place, my speech is intelligent.

I am Re himself, I am not to be ignored, I am not to be molested.

Thy father liveth for thee, O Son of Nut! I am thy son Horus, I see thy mysteries, and am crowned as King of the gods. I die not a second time in the Netherworld.

Royal sepulchre (possibly Thebes).

Oh thou who shinest forth from the Moon, thou who givest light from the Moon, let me come forth at large amid thy train, let me be revealed as one of those in glory. Let the Tuat be opened for me. Here am I: let me come forth upon this day, and be glorified. Let the glorified ones grant to me that I live and that mine adversaries be brought to me in bonds before the divine Circle; may the Genius of my mother be propitiated thereby, as I rise up upon my feet with a sceptre of gold in my hand, and lop off the limbs. May I rise up, a Babe [from between] the knees of Sothis, when they close together.

Here we have an expression of the Egyptians' fear of the dismemberment of their bodies after death. It was particularly important that the heart, being the seat of conscience and understanding, should not be taken away.

O ye gods who seize upon Hearts, and who pluck out the Whole Heart; and whose hands fashion anew the Heart of a person according to what he hath done; lo now, let that be forgiven to him by you.

Hail to you, O ye Lords of Everlasting Time and Eternity!

Let not my Heart be torn from me by your fingers.

Let not my Heart be fashioned anew according to all the evil things said against me.

For this Heart of mine is the Heart of the god of mighty names of the great god whose words are in his members, and who giveth free course to his Heart which is within him.

And most keen of insight is his Heart among the gods. Ho to me! Heart of mine; I am in possession of thee, I am thy master, and thou art by me; fall not away from me; I am the dictator to whom thou shalt obey in the Netherworld.

O Lion-god!

I am Unbu, and what I abominate is the block of execution.

Let not this Whole Heart of mine be torn from me by the divine Champions in Heliopolis!

O thou who clothest Osiris and hast seen Sutu:

O thou who turnest back after having smitten him, and hast accomplished the overthrow:

This Whole Heart of mine remaineth weeping over itself in presence of Osiris.

And this Whole Heart of mine is laid upon the tablets of Tmu, who guideth me to the caverns of Sutu and who giveth me back my Whole Heart which hath accomplished its desire in presence of the divine Circle which is in the Netherworld.

The sacrificial joint and the funereal raiment, let those who find them bury them.

Its strength proceedeth from him, it hath obtained it by prayer from him.

I have had granted to it and awarded to it the glow of heart at the hour of the god of the Broad Face, and have offered the sacrificial cakes in Hermopolis.

Let not this Whole Heart of mine be torn from me. It is I who entrust to you its place, and vehemently stir your Whole Hearts towards it in Sekhet-Hetepet and the years of triumph over all that in abhors and taking all provisions at thine appointed time from thine hand after thee.

Left: The Rosetta Stone

In 1799, while digging the foundations of a fort at Rosetta, in the Nile Delta, some French soldiers in Napoleon's army came across the black stone tablet known to history as the Rosetta Stone. It contains the text of a decree from 196 BC, written in Egyptian hieroglyphs and demotic, with a Greek translation. By comparing the three versions, the French scholar Champollion became the first European to decipher the hieroglyphs; thereafter Egyptian literature and inscriptions, which had been a mystery even to Egyptians since the beginning of the Christian era, became intelligible once again.

A remarkable passage in which the deceased identifies each part of his body with those of various deities.

Land of the Rod, of the White Crown of the Image, and the Pedestal of the gods.

I am the Babe. *(Said Four Times.)*

O Serpent Abur! Thou sayest this day, "The Block of Execution is furnished with what thou knowest," and thou art come to soil the Mighty One.

But I am he whose honours are abiding.

I am the Link, the god within the Tamarisk, who connecteth the Solar orb with Yesterday. *(Four Times.)*

I am Re, whose honours are abiding.

I am the Link, the god within the Tamarisk.

My course is the course of Re, and the course of Re is my course.

My hair is that of Nu.

My two eyes are those of Hathor,

My two ears those of Apuat,

My nose that of Chenti-chas,

My two lips those of Anubis,

My teeth those of Selkit,

My neck that of Isis, the Mighty,

My two hands those of the Soul most Mighty, Lord of Tattu,

My shoulders those of Neith, Mistress of Sais,

My back is that of Sut,

My phallus that of Osiris,

My liver is that of the Lords of Kher-âbat,

My knees those of the most Mighty one,

My belly and my back are those of Sechit,

My hinder parts are those of the Eye of Horus,

My legs and thighs those of Nut,

My feet those of Ptah,

My nails and bones those of the Living Uraei.

There is not a limb in me which is without a god. And Thoth is a protection to my flesh.

I shall not be grasped by my arms or seized

"The Magic Eye" (Tomb at Pashedu).

by my hands.

Not men or gods, or the glorified ones or the damned; not generations past, present, or future, shall inflict any injury upon me.

I am he who cometh forth and proceedeth, and whose name is unknown to man.

I am Yesterday, "Witness of Eternity" is my Name: the persistent traveller upon the heavenly highways which I survey. I am the Everlasting one.

I am felt and thought of as Khepera. I am the Crowned one.

I am the Dweller in the Eye and in the Egg. It is an attribute of mine that I live within them.

I am the Dweller in the Eye, even in its closing.

I am that by which it is supported.

I come forth and I rise up: I enter and I have life.

I am the Dweller in the Eye; my seat is upon my throne, and I sit conspicuously upon it.

I am Horus, who steppeth onwards through Eternity.

This brief text illustrate the importance of the funeral ritual of "opening the mouth" of the deceased. This ceremony was thought to enable the deceased to partake of food and drink in the Underworld. The "Egg in the unseen world" is the sun before sunrise.

He saith: Let my mouth be opened by Ptah, and let the muzzles which are upon my mouth be loosed by the god of my domain.

Then let Thoth come, full and equipped with Words of Power, and let him loose the muzzles of Sutu which are upon my mouth, and let Tmu lend a hand to fling them at the assailants.

Let my mouth be given to me. Let my mouth be opened by Ptah with that instrument of steel wherewith he openeth the mouths of the gods.

I am Sechit Uat'it who sitteth on the right side of Heaven: I am Sahit encircled by the Spirits of Heliopolis.

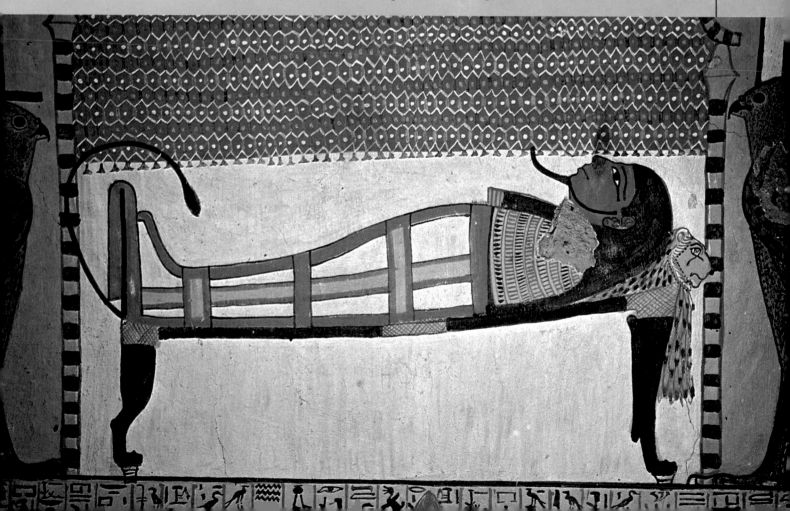

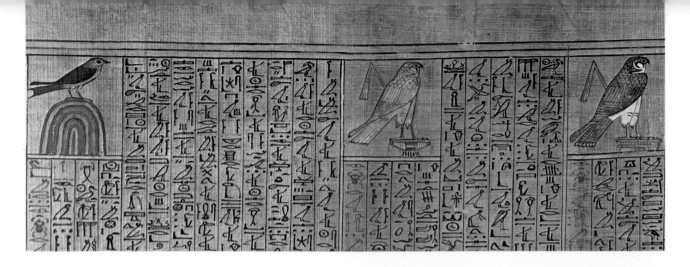

43-44-45 (Above)

"Transformation into a hawk of gold".

"Transformation into a divine hawk".

"Transformation into the serpent Sito". Sito is the primeval serpent god who encircles the world; he is sometimes shown, as here, with legs for greater ease when walking! Center: "Transformation into a crocodile". In this spell the deceased proclaims that he devours his prey like a savage beast. Right: "Transformation into Ptah". Ptah was the creator-god of Memphis.

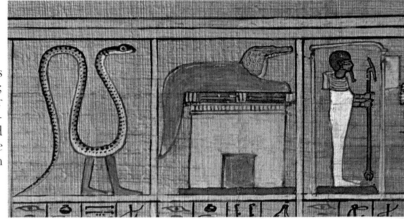

46-47-48 (Opposite)

"Transformation into a living soul". A ram, perhaps symbolizing Osiris, on a pedestal; on the right is an emblem for the *ba* soul.

"Transformation into a *Bennu* bird".

"Transformation into a heron".

49-50 (Below)

"Transformation into a lotus" (left), and "Transformation into the god who lightens the darkness".

60

51

"Of not dying a second time". Ani and Thuthu stand with hands raised in adoration before the god Thoth who sits on a pylonshaped pedestal.

52

The text accompanying this page and the next vignette is a hymn of praise to Osiris, the lord of Amenta. Ani and his wife stand, their hands raised in adoration, before a table of offerings, facing the great dead king and king of the dead, Osiris.

53

Osiris stands in a shrine on the hieroglyphic symbol for *maat*. Isis is behind him in her usual protective pose. The four Children of Horus stand facing Osiris on an open lotus flower. Osiris holds the usual emblems of royal and divine authority: the *was* scepter, the crook and the flail. Above the shrine is the Sokaris hawk guarded by thirteen cobras.

54

The Protestation of Innocence (also known as the Negative Confession). Ani addresses forty-two gods in turn, assuring each of them that he has not committed a particular sin; the number forty-two is thought to reflect the fact that there were as many administrative districts, or nomes, in Egypt. This chapter is commonly regarded as evidence of the high sense of moral responsibility of the ancient Egyptians, though some authors emphasize its magical nature, which was evidently thought to cancel out sins by the mere force of words.

Each column follows the same pattern. Top register: "Hail, thou (name of god)"; lower register: "(I have) not committed (name of each offense)". At either end of the hall is half of a folding door. The cornice at the top of this illustration bears a row of ostrich feathers, symbolic of *maat,* alternating with uraei. The figure in the middle is the Spirit of the Eternal Waters, his hands stretched out over the Eye of Horus and a pool of water. On the far right are two goddesses of law, Ani adoring Osiris, the trial of the conscience and the scribe-god Thoth with the ostrich feather of law.

55

"Deification of the parts of the body of the deceased". Here the deceased proclaims that each part of his body is actually that of some god, or, in the last two columns, the star Orion or the uraei. The four registers read as follows:

Top: "Is the (name of part of body)".
2nd: "Of Osiris-Ani triumphant".
3rd: "(Name of god)".
Bottom: Picture of god.

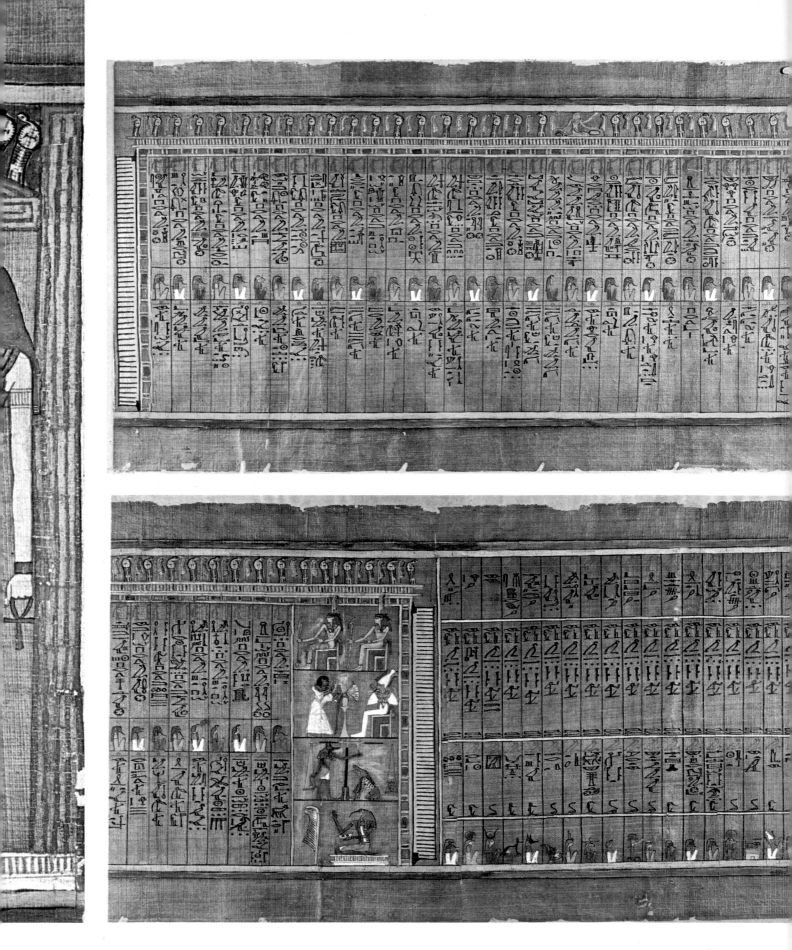

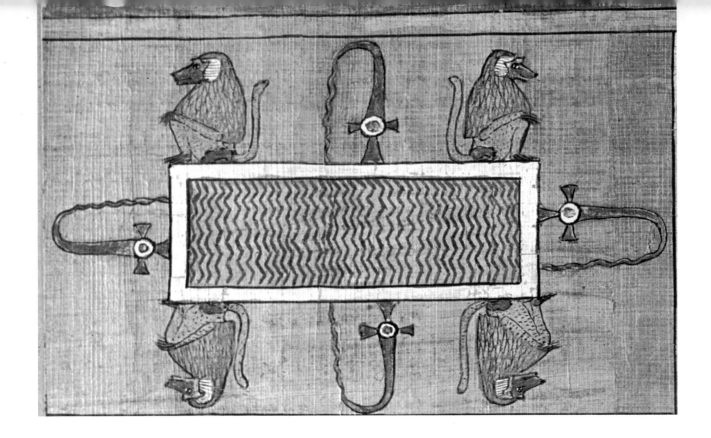

56

The scribe probably made a mistake at this point, as the text accompanying this vignette seems irrelevant to it. A similar vignette in the Papyrus of Nu (c. 1650 BC, one of the oldest illustrated copies of the Book of the Dead so far discovered) is shown with an other chapter in it the deceased, after glorifying the apes, the Spirits of the Dawn, "who make the gods contented by the flames of their mouths", appeals to them to let him into Restau, the passage to the Underworld. The apes then reply and the deceased proceeds further.

57

These four amulets were often placed with the mummy. From the left: "The *djed* of gold"; Ani promises to bring Osiris a *djed* of gold. "The buckle of cornelian". Ani here invokes the protection of Isis, whose symbol this is. "The heart of cornelian"; this is an incantation for the soul of Ani to come back to do the will of his *ka* or spiritual double. "The pillow"; the object in the vignette is a headrest. The deceased, being an Egyptian, must have been horrified at the slightest prospect of his body being mutilated,

as his hopes of eternal life would thereby be lost;
here he prays that his head may never be taken
away from him.

58

    Ani and wife in the customary pose of adoration,
as Ani prepares to enter the Egyptian equivalent
of the Elysian Fields, the Fields of Peace.

59

The vignette shows the mummy chamber, each
wall of which is decorated with a figure and
columns of hieroglyphs. In the middle is Anubis
watching over the mummy. The squares im-
mediately surrounding him contain the four
Children of Horus, Isis and Nephtys, a *djed*
column and Anubis on a pylon, with flail, *kherp*
scepter and two *menats*. The outer columns are
occupied by two bird-shaped souls, two flames
and two *ushabti*-figures. If Ani's name happens
to be called out in the Divine Roll-call, then the
ushabti will answer for him, "sowing fields, filling
channels with water and carrying sand". Each of
the figures in the vignette addresses the mummy,
offering to protect it.

60
"Sekhet-Hetepet (Fields of Peace) and going into and coming out of the Underworld". Ani adores the gods who dwell in Sekhet-Hetepet, and asks them to help him gain admittance so that he may "become a *khu,* drink, plow, reap, fight, make love, never be in a state of servitude and alway be in a position of authority therein". Vi-gnette, top register: Ani and his *khaibit* are introduced to Thoth by three gods; he is then shown paddling a boat and adressing a hawk figure; right, a mummy and three pools. 2nd: Ani at work in the fields, worshiping a *Bennu* bird and sitting holding a scepter; piles of corn, three *khus* and *kas* and three pools are also shown. 3rd: Ani plowing. Bottom: island with steps, two boats.

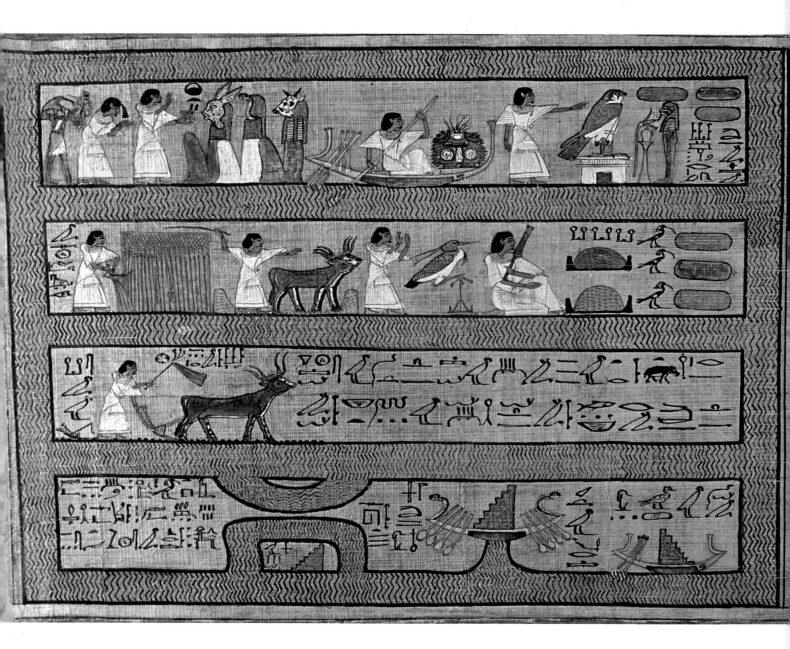

61

'Providing the deceased with food in the Under-world'. The extremely short text accompanying this vignette in the Papyrus of Ani contains an invocation to the sun-god Re In which Ani says he hopes he will be a *khu* in Amenta. He also

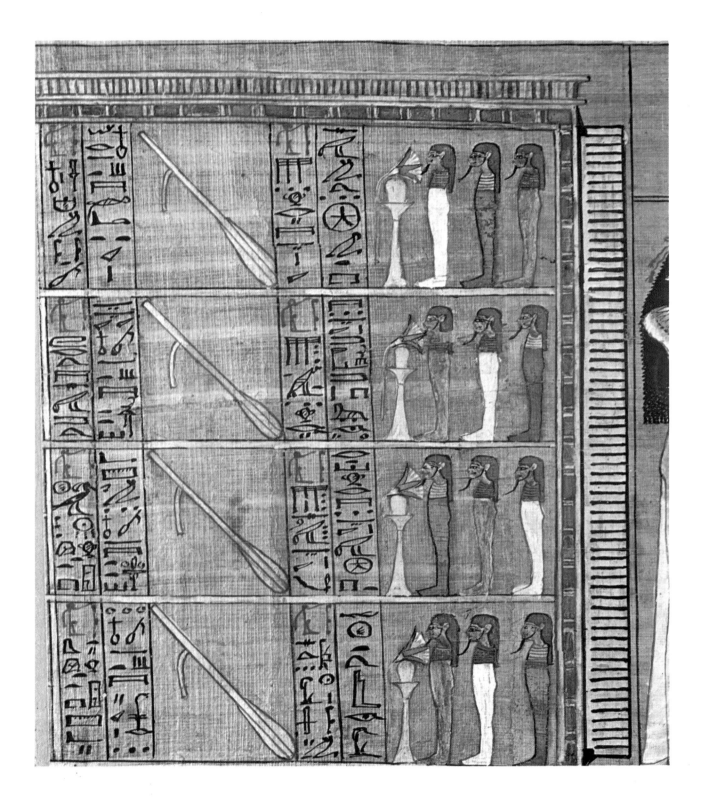

addresses prayers to the four Rudders of Heaven, symbolizing the four cardinal points. Vignette: Ani adoring the hawk-headed sun-god Re, who has a solar disk with a cobra on his head; the seven sacred cows and the bull symbolize sustenance for Ani in the hereafter. Next are shown the four Rudders of Heaven and four triads of gods.

62

'Praise to Hathor and Mehurt'. The deceased invokes the protection and help of Hathor in the Underworld, assuring her that during his lifetime on earth he did a great many things in her service. Vignettes: Ani and Thuthu in a pose of adoration before a table of offerings, facing the hawk-headed figure of Osiris-Seker (Seker = Sokaris, god of the necropolis, the center of whose cult was in Memphis), standing in a shrine holding the usual emblems of power. Behind him are Hathor, the hippopotamus goddess, and Mehurt, another form of the same deity, facing a table of offerings.

The exact nature of the object held by Hathor in her right hand is uncertain. Mehurt wears the Hathor crown and adornments, including the *menat*. She peers forth, thrugh a cluster of lotus flowers, from the mountain at the foot of which the tomb is situated.

The deceased, in a confident mood, identifies himself with the gods and feels assured of a smooth passage through the Underworld, possessing, as he does, the Words of Power.

I come forth victoriously against the adversaries.

I cleave the heaven, I open the horizon and I travel over the earth on foot. There come forward to me the Glorious and the Great ones, for I am furnished with numberless Words of Might.

I eat with my mouth, and I chew with my jaw; for, lo, I worship the god who is Lord of the Tuat, and that is given to me which endureth amid overthrow.

Here is the Osiris *N*.
O Eater of his arm: away from his path!

I am Re coming forth from the horizon against his adversary, who shall not be delivered from me.

I have stretched out my hand, as the Lord of the Crown, and lifted my feet.

I shall not be given up; my adversary shall fall before me; he hath been given up to me and shall not be delivered from me.

I rise up like Horus, I sit down as Ptah, I am victorious as Thoth, and powerful as Tmu: I walk upon my feet, I speak with my mouth, searching for him who hath been given up to me; he shall not be delivered from me.

This text refers to the remarkable institution of the ushabti *figures which were supposed to do hard physical toil on behalf of the deceased in the Underworld.*

O Statuette there! Should I be called and appointed to do any of the labours that are done in the Netherworld by a person according to his abilities, lo! all obstacles have been beaten down for thee; be thou counted for me at every moment, for planting the fields, for watering the soil, for conveying the sands of east and west.

Here am I, whithersoever thou callest me.

Here the deceased makes an important claim—that his names are hidden, and a perpetual secret. In other words, he likens himself to the gods.

Oh, One of Wax, who takest captive and seizest with violence, and livest upon those who are motionless! Let me not become motionless before thee, let me not be paralysed before thee, let not thy venoms enter into my limbs, for my limbs are the limbs of Tmu.

And if thou wouldst not be paralysed, let me not be paralysed.

Let not thy languors enter these limbs of mine.

I am the One who presideth over the pole of Heaven, and the powers of all the gods are my powers.

I am he, whose names are hidden, and whose abodes are mysterious for all eternity.

It is I who proceed from Tmu, and I am safe and sound.

The Theban Necropolis: decoration of the chapel at Anubis.

Below:
Pilasters embellished in a lotus-flower pattern, part of the remains of the great Temple to Amon at Karnak.

Left:
This allegory, depicted on the stele of the "Lady Tuth-Shena", has been the object of widely varied and thus somewhat dubious interpretations.

One of the most important passages in the "Book of the Dead". The deceased here displays the requisite level of knowledge about divine matters, and is accordingly allowed to proceed further through the Underworld.

I am he who closeth and he who openeth, and I am but One.

I am Re at his first appearance.

I am the great god, self-produced;

His Names together compose the cycle of the gods;

Resistless is he among the gods.

I, who am Osiris, am Yesterday and the kinsman of the Morrow.

A scene of strife arose among the gods when I gave the command.

Amenta is the scene of strife among the gods.

I know the name of the great god who is here.

Herald of Re is his name.

I am the great Heron who is in Heliopolis, who presideth over the account of whatsoever is and of that which cometh into being.,

Who is that? It is Osiris who presideth over the account of all that is and all that cometh into being, that is Endless Time and Eternity. Endless Time is Day and Eternity is Night.

I am Amsu in his manifestations; there have been given to me the Two Feathers upon my head.

Who is that, and what are his Feathers? It is Horus, the avenger of his father, and the Two Feathers are the Uræi upon the forehead of his

Removal of a coffin.

father Tmu.

I have alighted upon my Land, and I come from my own Place.

What is that? It is the Horizon of my father Tmu.

All defects are done away, all deficiencies are removed, and all that was wrong in me is cast forth.

I am purified at the two great and mighty Lakes at Sutenhunen, which purify the offerings which living men present to the great god who is there.

Who is that? It is Re himself.

Which are the two great and mighty Lakes? The Lake of Natron and the Lake of Maat.

I advance over the roads, which I know, and my face is one the Land of Maat.

What is that? The road upon which father Tmu advanceth, when he goeth to the Field of Aarru, approaching to the land of Spirits in Heaven.

I come forth through the T'eser gate.

What is that? This gate of the gods is Haukar. It is the gate and the two doors and openings, through which father Tmu issueth to the Eastern Horizon of Heaven.

O ye who have gone before! Let me grasp your hands, me who become one of you.

Who are they? Those who have gone before are Hu and Sau. May I be with their father Tmu, throughout the course of each day.

I make full the Eye when it waxeth dim on the day of battle between the two Opponents.

The deceased continues to identify the various gods, while invoking their aid. The term "possessors of maat" refers to the gods: their function was, therefore, that of maintaining order, truth, stability, justice and the other notions which were implied by maat.

What is that? The battle of the two Opponents is the day upon which Horus fighteth with Sut, when he flingeth his filth upon the face of Horus, and when Horus seizeth upon the genitals of Sut, for it is Horus who doeth this with his own fingers.

I lift up the hairy net from the Eye at the period of its distress.

What is that? The right Eye of Re in the period of its distress when he giveth it free course, and it is Thoth who lifteth up the net from it.

I see Re, when he is born from Yesterday, at the dugs of the Mehurit cows? His course is my course, and conversely mine is his.

What is that? Re and his births from Yesterday at the dugs of the Mehurit cows? It is the figure of the Eye of Re, at his daily birth. And Mehurit is the Eye.

I am one of those who are in the train of Horus.

What is that — 'one of those in the train of Horus'? Said with reference to whom his Lord loveth.

Hail, ye possessors of *maat*, divine Powers attached to Osiris, who deal destruction to falsehood, ye who are in the train of Hotepeschaus, grant me that I may come to you. Do ye away the wrong which is me, as ye have done to the Seven Glorious ones, who follow after the Coffined one, and whose places Anubis hath fixed on that day of "Come thou hither"!

Hotepeschaus is the divine Flame which is assigned to Osiris for burning the souls of his adversaries. I know the names of the Seven Glorious ones who follow the Coffined one, and whose places Anubis hath fixed on the day of 'Come thou hither.' The leader of this divine company.

'An-ar-ef, the Great' is his name; 2, Kat-kat; 3, the Burning Bull, who liveth in his fire; 4, the Red-eyed one in the House of Gauze; 5, Fieryface which turneth backwards; 6, Dark Face in its hour; 7, Seer in the Night.

I am he whose Soul resideth in a pair of gods.

It is Osiris, as he cometh to Tattu, and there findeth the soul of Re; each embraceth the other, and becometh Two Souls.

The pair of gods are Horus, the Avenger of his Father, and Horus, the Prince of the City of Blindness.

I am the great Cat, who frequenteth the Persea tree in Heliopolis, on that night of battle wherein is effected the defeat of the Sebau, and that day upon which the adversaries of the Inviolate god are exterminated.

Who is that great Cat? It is Re himself. For Sau said, He is the likeness (Maàu) of that which he hath created, and his name became that of Cat (Maàu).

The night of conflict is the defeat of the children of Failure at Elephantine. There was conflict in the entire universe, in heaven and upon the earth.

He who frequenteth the Persea tree is he who regulateth the children of Failure, and that which they do.

O Re, in thine Egg, who risest up in thine orb, and shinest from thine Horizon, and swimmest over the firmament without a peer, and sailest over the sky; whose mouth sendeth forth breezes of flame, lightening up the Two Earths with thy glories, do thou deliver N from that god whose attributes are hidden, whose eyebrows are as the arms of the Balance upon that day when outrage is brought to account, and each wrong is tied up to its separate block of settlement.

The deceased combines boasting of his own supernatural powers with humble pleas for divine assistance.

The god whose eyebrows are as the arms of the Balance is "he who lifteth up his arm."

Deliver me from those Wardens of the Passages with hurtful fingers, attendant upon Osiris.

The Wardens of Osiris are the Powers who keep off the forces of the adversaries of Re.

May your knives not get hold of me; may I not fall into your shambles, for I know your names; my course upon earth is with Re and my fair goal is with Osiris. Let not your offerings be in my disfavour, oh ye god upon your altars! I am one of those who follow the Master, a keeper of the writ of Khepera.

I fly like a Hawk, I cackle like the *Smen-Goose*, I move eternally like Nehebkau.

Oh Tmu who art in the Great Dwelling, Sovereign of all the gods, deliver me from that god who liveth upon the damned; whose face is that of a hound, but whose skin is that of a man; at that angle of the pool of fire; devouring shades, digesting human hearts and voiding ordure. One seeth him not.

This god whose face is that of a hound and whose skin is that of a man: Eternal Devourer is his name.

Oh Fearful one, who art over the Two Earths, Red god who orderest the block of execution; to whom is given the Double Crown and Enjoyment as Prince of Sutenhunen.

It is Osiris to whom was ordained the Leadership among the gods, upon that day when the Two Earths were united before the Inviolate god.

The junction of the Two Earths is the head of the coffin of Osiris [whose father is Re] the beneficent Soul in Sutenhunen, the giver of food and the destroyer of wrong, who hath determined the paths of eternity.

It is Re himself.

Deliver me from that god who seizeth upon souls, who consumed all filth and corruption in the darkness or in the light: all those who fear him are in powerless condition.

This god is Sut.

Oh Khepera, who are in the midst of thy bark and whose body is the cycle of the gods for ever; deliver me from those inquisitorial Wardens to whom the Inviolate god, of Glorious Attributes, hath given guard over his adversaries, and the infliction of slaughter in the place of annihilation, from whose guard there is no escape. May I not fall under your knives, may I not sit within your dungeons, may I not come to your places of extermination, may I not fall into your pits; may there be done to me none of those things which the gods abominate; for I have passed through the place of purification in the middle of the Meskat, for which are given the Mesit and the Tehenit cakes in Tanenit.

The Meskat is the place of scourging in Sutenhunen, the Tehenit is the Eye of Horus... Tanenit is the resting place of Osiris.

The Papyrus of Hunefer *(c. 1370 B.C.)*

1

Hymn of praise to Re as he rises in the East. Hunefer, the royal scribe, stands with his hands raised in adoration of the rising sun; he is followed by his wife Nasha, who holds a lotus-flower and a Hathor-headed sistrum. Below the vault of heaven stands Re-Harmakhis, in the form of a hawk with a solar disk surrounded by a cobra. The Spirits of the Dawn, the apes, worship on either side. Beneath is the *djed* column with a pair of arms holding a crook and a flail, symbols of power and rule, and Isis and Nephthys.

2

"Hymn of praise to Osiris" and speech of Thoth. Hunefer and his wife stand adoring Thoth who holds the emblem of life flanked by two *was* scepters. The vertical line of hieroglyphs listing Hunefer's titles is of particular interest because it tells us the date of the papyrus: the cartouche is that of Seti I, whose reign began about the year 1370 BC.

3

The Weighing of the Heart. Anubis leads Hunefer into the Hall of Double Maat, where his heart (in other words, his conscience) is weighed against the feather of order, justice and truth. Anubis checks the tongue of the balance, while the monster known as the "Eater of the Dead" looks on. Thoth records the result. Horus then leads Hunefer towards the shrine in which Osiris sits on a throne; behind him are his sisters Isis and Nephthys; from the pool of water beneath the throne rises a lotus flower on which the four Children of Horus stand facing the great god. The winged *udjat* carries a *shen* emblem and a feather.

5

"Giving a mouth to the deceased". Here we see the ceremonies at the tomb, including the ceremony of the "opening of the mouth". The priest wearing the leopard skin holds a censer and a libation vase; the other two are preparing to

4

There are the "Chapters of coming forth by day". This is a prayer for the divine favor in the after-life—including, characteristically, "cakes and ale"—followed by a part of the ritual to be performed before the interment of the mummy. The vignette shows the funeral procession. A shrine and the bier bearing Hunefer's mummy on a funeral boat ar towed by oxen towards the tomb; both ave figures of Anubis on them. A priest burns incense and pours libations before the bier. The next group of figures consists of al priest reading from a scroll, a party of mourners and a servant carrying objects belonging to Hunefer.

touch the eyes and mouth of the deceased with special instruments, shaped like an adze and a ram-headed serpent (the *ur-hekau*). There is a table of offerings between them. Next to the tomb and the funerary stele is the mummy of Hunefer, supported by Anubis, and a pair of female mourners.

6-7

"*Praises and glorification of entering and leaving the Underworld... transformatins, playing drafts...*". Like the version of the same chapter in the Papyrus of Ani, this is a kind of theological question-and-answer test which Hunefer has to pass before being allowed to proceed further in the Underworld. The vignettes are based on the text of this chapter which is given in this papyrus, though the latter part of the chapter is not illustrated. The Papyrus of Ani, for example, has vignettes of Khepera, Tem, the liongod Rehu and Uatchit, the

Lady of Flame, all corresponding to passages in the text; the Papyrus of Hunefer stops with the scene in which the Cat (i.e., Re) slays the serpent. Here we see Hunefer walking simultaneously in opposite directions from the symbol of Amenta, thus showing that he is free to enter and leave the Underworld; in the next scene he is playing drafts—another manifestation of the desired freedom of the deceased.

The soul of Hunefer; Hunefer adoring the two lions which symbolize Yesterday and Today (Osiris and Re); between them is the horizon with the solar disk.

8-9-10 (Above)

Osiris seated with the flail and crook, emblems of power, on his knees; Hunefer kneeling at a table of offerings, before a *Bennu* bird.

A hawk-headed god wearing the Double Crown.

Hunefer's mummy lying on a bier guarded by the souls of Isis and Nephthys.

Hunefer kneeling before two serpent goddesses; a table of offerings; a god holding out his hand over the Eye of Horus; the Spirit of the Eternal Waters holding out his hand over a lake.

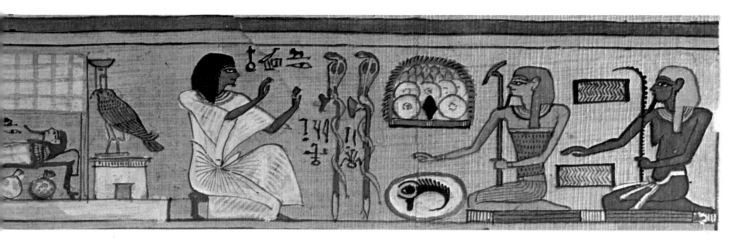

11 (Left)

Hunefer and his wife worshiping the gods of Amenta; a pylon leading to Amenta; four gods, including **Re**; Thoth kneels before Mehurt, holding an *udjat*.

12-13 (Opposite and below)

Hunefer worships Re, whose head emerges from a funeral chest and who is surrounded by the four **Children of Horus**, his "sovereign princes".

Hunefer kneeling before seven gods, mentioned in the text as being the protectors of Osiris. Each god is armed with a knife.

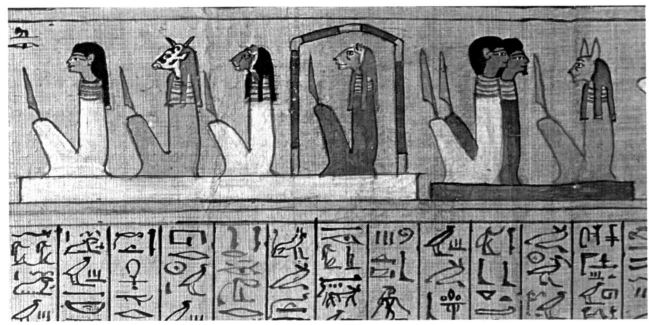

14

Hunefer continues to identify correctly the gods whose mission it is to protect Osiris. Here he is seen kneeling before five ram-headed gods.

15

The Cat, symbolic of Re, cuts off the head of the Serpent of Darkness, Apophis. Hunefer identifies himself with the Cat, as having defeated the enemies of Re.

The deceased invoke the divine assistance.

Tmu buildeth thy dwelling, the Lion-faced god layeth the foundation of thy house, as he goeth his round. Horus offereth purification and Sut giveth might, and conversely.

I have come upon this earth and with my two feet taken possession. I am Tmu and I come from my own Place.

Back, oh Lion with dazzling mouth, and with head bent forwards, retreating before me and my might.

I am Isis and thou findest me as I drop upon my face the hair which falleth loosely on my brow.

I was conceived by Isis and begotten by Nephthys. Isis destroyeth what in me is wrong, and Nephthys loppeth off that which is rebellious.

Dread cometh in my train and Might is in my hands. Numberless are the hands who cling fast to me. The dead ones and the living come to me. I defeat the clients of mine adversaries, and spoil those whose hands are darkened.

I have made an agreeable alliance. I have created the inhabitants of Kher-âbat and those of Heliopolis. And every god is in fear before the Terrible, the Almighty one.

I avenge every god against his oppressor, at whom I shoot my arrows when he appeareth.

I live according to my will.

I am Uatchit, the Fiery one.

And woe to them who mount up against me! What is this? "Of unknown attributes, which Hemen hath given" is the name of the Funereal Chest. "The Witness of that which is lifted" is the name of the Shrine.

The Lion with dazzling mouth and with head bent forwards is the Phallus of Osiris [*otherwise* of Re.

And I who drop the hair which hath loosely fallen upon my brow—I am Isis, when she concealeth herself; she hath let fall her hair over herself.

Uatchit the Fiery is the Eye of Re.

They who mount up against me, woe to them, they are the associates of Sut as they approach.

Here we have the opening of the famous "Protestation of Innocence" (Negative Confession). This page was very often chosen for inclusion in the texts of papyri of the Book of the Dead. It occurs in the papyri of Ani and Hunefer.

Said on arriving at the Hall of Righteousness, that *N* may be loosed from all the sins which he hath committed and that he may look upon the divine countenances.

He saith: Hail to thee, mighty god, lord of Righteousness!

I am come to thee, oh my Lord: I have brought myself that I may look upon thy glory. I know thee, and I know the names of the Forty-two gods who make their appearance with thee in the Hall of Righteousness; devouring those who harbour mischief, and swallowing their blood, upon the Day of the searching examination in presence of Unneferu.

Verily, Thou of the Pair of Eyes, 'Lord of Righteousness' is thy name.

Here am I; I am come to thee; I bring to thee Right and have put a stop to Wrong.

I am not a doer of wrong to men.

I am not one who slayeth his kindred.

I am not one who telleth lies instead of truth.

I am not conscious of treason.

I am not a doer of mischief.

I do not exact as the firstfruits of each day more work than should be done for me.

My name cometh not to the Bark of the god who is at the Helm.

I am not a transgressor against the god.

I am not a tale-bearer.

I am not a detractor.

I am not a doer of that which the gods abhor.

View of the grand entrance hall in the Temple to Hathor at Denderah.

I hurt no servant with his master.
I cause no famine.
I cause not weeping.
I am not a murderer.
I give not orders for murder.
I cause not suffering to men.
I reduce not the offerings in the temples.
I lessen not the cakes of the gods.
I rob not the dead of their funereal food.
I am not an adulterer.
I am undefiled in the Sanctuary of the god of my domain.
I neither increase nor diminish the measures of grain.
I am not one who shorteneth the palm's length.
I am not one who cutteth short the field's measure.
I put not pressure upon the beam of the balance.
I tamper not with the tongue of the balance.
I snatch not the milk from the mouth of infants.
I drive not the cattle from their pastures.
I net not the birds of the manors of the gods.
I catch not the fish of their ponds.
I stop not the water at its appointed time.
I divide not an arm of the water in its course.
I extinguish not the lamp during its appointed time.
I do not defraud the Divine Circle of their sacrificial joints.

The "Protestation of Innocence", continued. It is interesting to note that many of the offenses listed involved the theft of sacred property. Thanks to liberal tax exemptions and other benefits, the temples, particularly those of Thebes about the time of Ani, were enormously rich.

I drive not away the cattle of the sacred estate.
I stop not a god when he cometh forth.
I am pure, I am pure, I am pure, I am pure.
My purity is that of the Great Bennu in Sutenhunen, for I am the Nose of the Lord of Air, who giveth life to all mortals; on the day when the Eye is full in Annu, on the last day of Mechir; in presence of the Lord of this land.
And I am one who see the fulness of the Eye in Annu, let no harm come to me in this land, in the Hall of Righteousness; because I know the names of those gods who make their appearance in it.

1. Oh thou of long strides, who makest thine appearance in Annu; I am not a doer of wrong.
2. Oh thou who holdest the fire, and makest thine appearance in Kher-àba; I am not a man of violence.
3. Oh thou of the Nose, who makest thine appearance at Khemunnu; I am not evil minded.
4. Oh Eater of the Shadow, who makest thine appearance at Elephantine; I am not rapacious.
5. Oh thou Facing-backward god, who makest thine appearance at Re-Stau; I am not a slayer of men.
6. Oh thou of Lion form, who makest thine appearance in Heaven; I am not fraudulent in measures of grain.
7. Oh thou whose eyes pierce like swords, who makest thine appearance in Sechem; I commit no fraud.
8. Oh thou of fiery face, whose motion is backwards; I am not a robber of sacred property.
9. Oh Breaker of bones, who makest thine appearance in Sutenhunen; I am not a teller of lies.
10. Oh thou who orderest the flame, who makest thine appearance in Memphis; I am not a robber of food.
11. Oh thou of the Two Caverns, who makest thine appearance in Memphis; I am not sluggish.
12. Oh thou of the Bright Teeth, who makest thine appearance in the Unseen Land; I am not a transgressor.
13. Oh Eater of Blood, who makest thine appearance at the Block; I have not slaughtered the sacred animals.

Haradkty of Tutankhamen.

Detail from bas-relief of the pylon at the entrance to the Temple at Luxor.

94

14. Oh Eater of Livers, who makest thine appearance at Mâbit; I deal not fraudulently.

15. Oh Lord of Righteousness, who makest thine appearance in the place of Righteousness; I am not a land-grabber.

16. Oh thou who turnest backwards, who makest thine appearance in Bubastis; I am not an eaves-dropper.

17. Oh Aati, who makest thine appearance at Annu; I am not one of prating tongue.

18. Oh Tutu, who makest thine appearance in Ati; I trouble myself only with my own affairs.

19. Oh Uammetu, who makest thine appearance at the Block; I commit not adultery with another's wife.

20. Oh Maa-antu-f, who makest thine appearance in Pa-Amsu, I am not unchaste with any one.

21. Oh thou who art above Princes, and who makest thine appearance in Amu; I do not cause terrors.

22. Oh Chemiu, who makest thine appearance in Kauu; I am not a transgressor.

23. Oh thou who raisest thy voice, and makest thine appearance in Urit; I am not hot of speech.

24. Oh divine Babe, who makest thy appearance in Annu; I lend not a deaf ear to the words of Righteousness.

25. Oh high-voiced one, who makest thy appearance in Unsit; I am not boisterous in behaviour.

26. Oh Basit, who makest thine appearance at the Shetait; I am not the cause of weeping to any.

27. Oh thou whose face is behind thee, and who makest thine appearance at thy cavern; I am not given to unnatural lust.

28. Oh thou, hot of foot, who makest thy appearance at even; I indulge not in anger.

29. Oh Kenemtu, who makest thine appearance in Kenemit; I am not given to cursing.

30. Oh thou who carriest thine own offering, and makest thine appearance in Syut; I am not of aggressive hand.

31. Oh thou who hast different faces, and makest thine appearance in Net'efit; I am not one of inconstant mind.

32. Oh Busy one, who makest thine appearance at Utenit; I do not steal the skins of the sacred animals.

33. Oh thou Horned one, who markest thine appearance at Sais I am not noisy in my speech.

The "Protestation of Innocence", continued. Once the deceased has completed listing all the sins he has not committed, he addresses the gods of the Underworld (Tuat). Note that he begins by assuring them that he knows their names. A person's name was thought to have special magic significance, while knowledge of the names of the gods was crucial to survival after death.

34. Oh Nefertmu, who makest thine appearance in Memphis; I am neither a liar nor a doer of mischief.

35. Oh Tem-sepu, who makest thine appearance in Tattu; I am not one who curseth the king.

36. Oh thou wo doest according to thine own will, and makest thine appearance in Tebuu; I put no check upon the water in its flow.

37. Oh Striker, who makest thine appearance in Heaven; I am not one of loud voice.

38. Oh thou who makest mortals to flourish, and who makest thine appearance at Sais; I curse not a god.

39. Oh thou of beautiful shoulder, who makest thine appearance at...; I am not swollen with pride.

40. Oh Neheb-kau, who makest thy appearance at thy cavern; I have no unjust preferences.

41. Oh thou of raised head, who makest thine appearance at thy cavern; I have no strong desire except for my own property.

42. Oh thou who liftest an arm, and who makest thine appearance in the Netherworld, I do not that which offendeth the god of my domain.

The Papyrus
of Anhaï *(c. 1100 B.C.)*

1

Hymn to Re-Harmakhis ("horizon") when he rises. After reciting the titles of Re, Anhai invokes his favors, asking, for example, that she may be given food, drink and offerings in the Underworld and admitted to the company of the gods, and that her body may be taken to the province of Thebes.

Vignette: Anhai, a member of the College of Amun-Re at Thebes, stands with hands raised in adoration of the sun-god Re; before her is a table of offerings. She holds a sistrum and flowers in her left hand. Unlike Thuthu, wife of Ani, and Nasha, wife of Hunefer, she is wearing an almost transparent garment. The hawk with solar disk on its head symbolizes the rising sun. Beneath it is the symbol of the West, rising from a mountain, though this symbol is often associated with the West and the setting sun. On either side of the sun is a winged Eye of Horus with the *shen* symbol and a feather. Among the figures worshiping the sun are four apes (the Spirits of the Dawn), Isis and Nephthys, and the bird-shaped soul of Anhai. Above each bird is Anhai's name, spelt, for reasons of symmetry, in opposite directions.

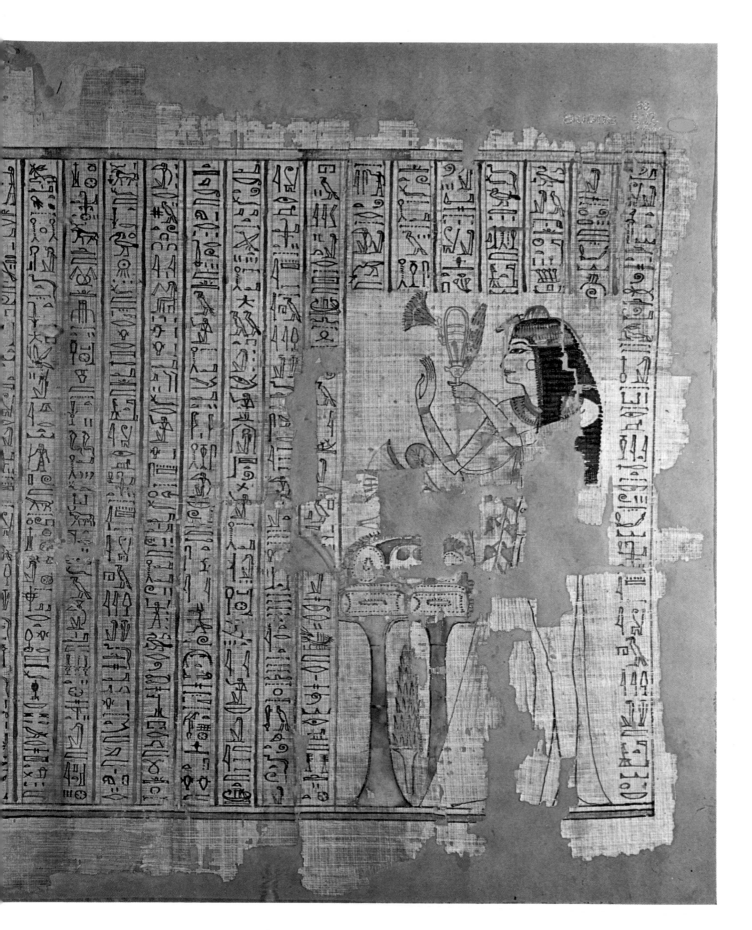

2

Invocations of Osiris by Horus and Thoth. They list the things they have done for the great god of the dead, and beg him to be favorable to Anhai. Horus leads Anhai towards the pylons through which she must pass in order to reach Osiris.

"Passing through the secret pylons of the house of Osiris". Anhai, of course, correctly names the animal-headed gods guarding the pylons and is allowed to pass. She eventually finds herself standing at a table of offerings at the entrance to the Hall of Double *Maat* (left). Her hands are raised in adoration of the goddess Maat, who appears in the next illustration.

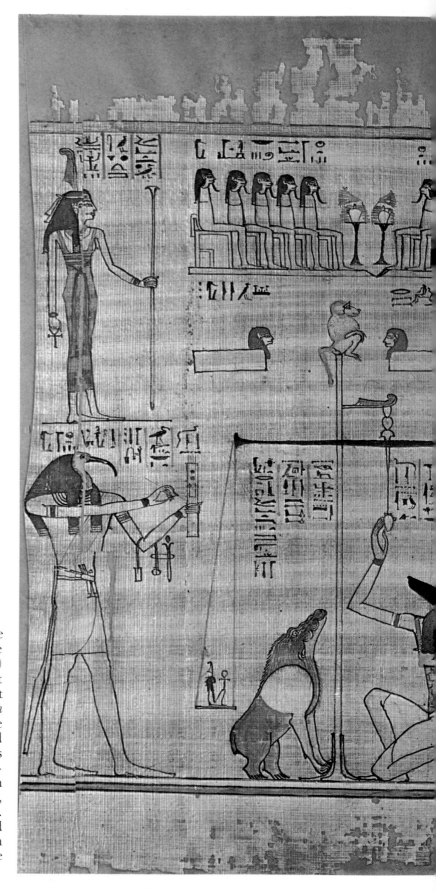

4

The Weighing of the Heart of the Dead. The goddess Maat (to left) stands at the entrance to the Hall of Double *Maat*. Horus (center) leads Anhai to the scales where her heart (right pan of the scales) will be weighed against Maat (figure with ostrich feather and *ankh* sign). Above, a company of gods sits before offering tables. Lower left: Thoth, symbolized also by the ape at the top of the scales, records the result of the trial. Right: Maat, accompanied by Amentit, who also wears an ostrich feather, raises her hands jubilantly, welcoming the now "triumphant" Anhai. Note that, in contrast to the Papyri of Ani and Hunefer, the vignettes of this papyrus contain virtually no picture of Osiris, even in the important judgment scene.

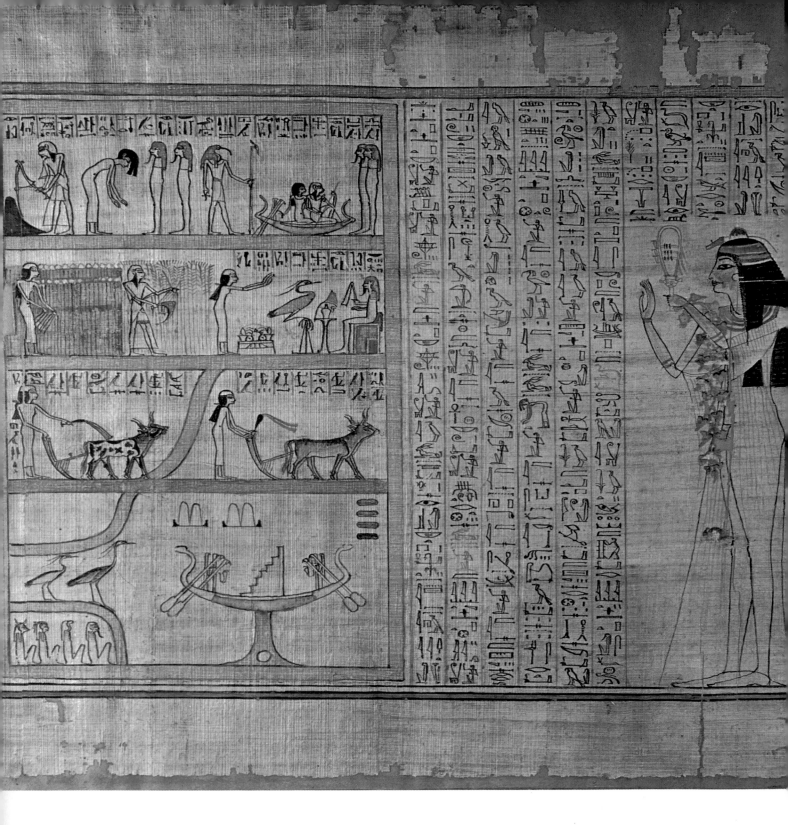

5

"Sekhet-Hetepet", the Fields of Peace. Anhai, with flowers and sistrum, in characteristic reverent pose. Top register: a male figure digging on a moutain; Anhai bowing before three goddesses; Thoth; Anhai in a boat with a man; two gods. 2nd: Anhai working in the fields with a man, perhaps her husband; Anhai in posture of adoration before a *Bennu* bird, some offerings and goddesses of the Underworld. 3rd: Anhai plowing a field on either side of a stream. 4th: A boat with steps, perhaps symbolizing the Primeval Mound; two islands, one of them with four gods of the Fields of Peace, and two *Bennu* birds on the bank of the stream.

6

A triple deity, Ptah-Seker-Osiris, combining the main gods of creation, death and the after-life, seated within a shrine. An animal's skin, with blood dripping from it, hangs on a pole before the throne. The brief texts, not part of any chapter of the Book of the Dead, are a welcoming address by the goddesses of southern and northern Egypt (top and bottom right, respectively), and some laudatory titles of the triple deity.

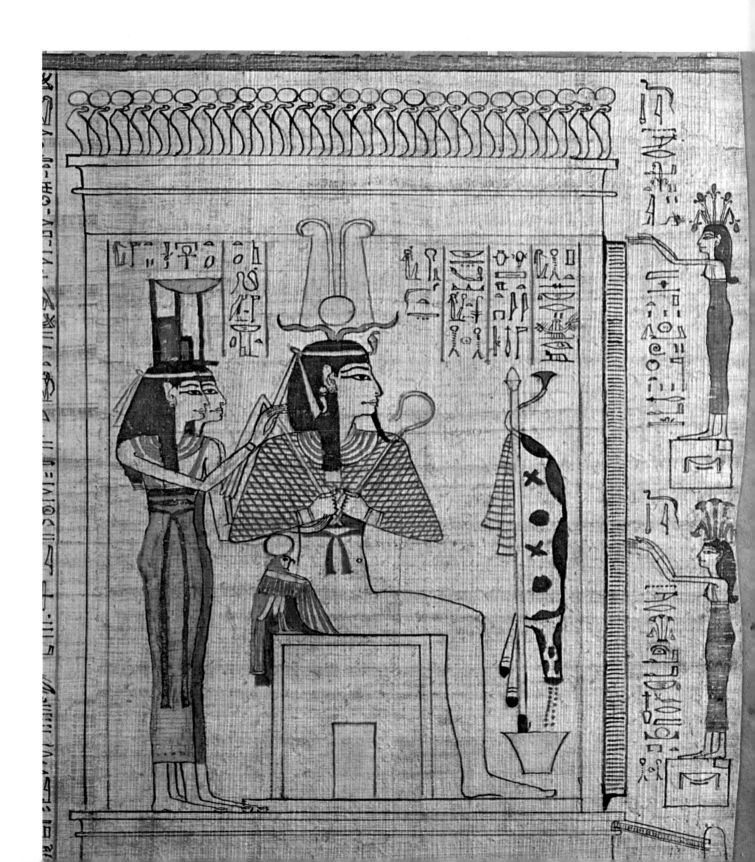

7

The Protestation of Innocence, with introduction. Anhai assures forty-two gods that she has not committed certain sins, such as stealing cakes from the gods, acting wickedly, etc., and, an interesting reflection on the Egyptians' use of irrigation rather than rainfall for agriculture, she denies ever having cut the banks of the running stream. In the top register the text reads: "Hail (name of god), who comest forth from (name of place); hail (name of second god) who comest forth from (name of second place). Lower register: "I have not (name of first offense) or (name of second offense)". On the far right Thoth with a scribe's palette; a hawkheaded figure checks the accuracy of the balance, the pans of which are empty; the goddess Maat.

8

Brief prayers to the gods on behalf of Anhai. Far-right, Osiris-Anhai in characteristic pose of adoration. Center: mummy of Anhai at top of double staircase of Hermopolis, venerated by ram-headed gods on either side. The eight disks above the staircase represent the eight great cosmic gods of the city. Left: the creation, a scene not from the Book of the Dead. Nu holds up the boat of the sun containing seven deities, above whom are a beetle (symbolic of birth and dawn) and the solar disk. The two figures shown upside down are Osiris and Nut.

The egyptian religious imagination is often well beyond the reach of the rational western mind. As happens frequently in the book of the dead, the deceased here not only invokes the aid of the gods, both major and minor, but actually proclaims his identity with them. He hopes, evidently, to bluff his way past the obstacles and dangers of the Underworld.

I have instituted the throne of which I am the master.

As regards my mouth: whether in speech or in silence, I am right and fair.

As regards my attributes: I hasten headlong, I the god Unen, with all that pertaineth to me, hour proceeding from hour, the One proceeding from the One, in my course.

I am the Dweller in the Eye; no evil or calamitous things befall me.

It is I who open the gates of Heaven; it is I who am master of the throne, and who open the series of births upon this day.

I am the Babe, who treadeth his path of Yesterday.

I am "This Day" to generation of men after generation.

I am he who giveth you stableness for eternity, whether ye be in heaven or upon earth; in the South, in the North, in the West, in the East—and the fear of me is upon you.

I am he who fashioneth with his eye, and who dieth not a second time.

A moment of mine belongeth to you, but my attributes belong to my own domain.

I am the Unknown one, but the gods of Ruddy Countenance belong to me.

I am the Gladsome one, and no time hath been found, but served to create for me the Heaven and the increase of Earth, and the increase of their offspring.

They sever and join not—they sever my name from all evil things, according to the words which I say unto you.

It is I who rise up and shine forth; strength proceeding from strength, the One proceeding from the One.

There is not a day devoid of that which belongeth to it; for ever and for ever.

I am Unbu, who proceedeth from Nu, and my mother is Nut.

O thou who hast set me in motion! for I was motionless, a mighty link within the close of Yesterday; my present activity is a link within the close of my hand.

I am not known, but I am one who knoweth thee.

I am not to be grasped, but I am one who graspeth thee.

[Oh Dweller in the Egg! Oh Dweller in the Egg!]

I am Horus, Prince of Eternity, a fire before your faces, which inflameth your hearts towards me.

I am master of my throne and I pass onwards. The present time is the path which I have opened, and I have set myself free from all things evil.

I am the golden Cynocephalus, three palms in height, without legs or arms in the Temple of Ptah; and my course is the course of the golden Cynocephalus, three palms in height, without legs or arms in the Temple of Ptah.

This passage from the protestation of innocence resembles in both tone and content certain parts of the hebrew psalms: the deceased claims to have lived a life of virtue and purity, while at the same time pleading for the divine assistance.

Behold me: I am come to you, void of wrong, without fraud, a harmless one: let me not be declared guilty; let not the issue be against me.

I subsist upon Righteousness: I sate myself with uprightness of heart: I have done that which man prescribeth and that which pleaseth the gods.

I have propitiated the god with that which he loveth. I have given bread to the hungry, water to the thirsty, clothes to the naked, a boat to the shipwrecked. I have made

Mummification.

oblations to the gods and funeral offerings to the departed: deliver me therefore: protect me therefore: and report not against me in presence of the great god.

I am one whose mouth is pure, and whose hands are pure, to whom there is said "Come, come in peace", by those who look upon him.

For I have listened to the words which were spoken by the Ass and the Cat in the house of Hept-ro.

And I have undergone the inspection of the god Whose face is behind him, who awardeth my verdict, so that I may behold what the Persea tree covereth in Restau.

I am one who glorifieth the gods and who knoweth the things which concern them.

I am come and am awaiting that inquisition be made of Rightfulness and that the Balance be set upon its stand within the bower of amaranth.

O thou who art exalted upon thy pedestal and who callest thy name, Lord of Air: deliver me from those messengers of thine who inflict disasters and bring about mishaps. No covering have they upon their faces.

For I have done the Righteousness of a Lord of Righteousness.

I have made myself pure: my front parts are washed, my back parts are pure, and my inwards steeped in the Tank of Righteousness. There is not a limb in me which is void of Righteousness.

I purify me in the Southern Tank, and I rest me at the northern lake, in the Garden of Grasshoppers.

The Boatmen of Re purify them there at this hour of the night or day and the hearts of the gods are appeased when I pass through it by night or by day.

In these spells the deceased, while describing the kind of after-life to which he aspires, expresses a strongly-felt fear which appears frequently in the Book of the Dead: the fear of being reduced to eating and drinking one's own waste matter.

I execrate, I execrate, I do not eat it.

That which I execrate is dirt. I eat it not, that I may appease my Genius.

Let it not fall upon me; let me not approach it with my hands, let me not tread upon it with my sandals.

Henceforth let me live upon corn in your presence, ye gods, and let there come one who

Left: Dead man's mummy presented to his wife and child as priests gesture with ritual objects.
Opposite: A comparable scene.

bringeth to me that I may feed from those seven loaves which he hath brought for Horus and upon the loaves for Thoth.

"What willst thou eat?" say the gods to him.

Let me eat under the Sycamore of Hathor the Sovereign, and let my turn be given to me among those who rest there.

And let me manage the fields in Tattu and prosper in Heliopolis.

And let me feed upon the bread of the white corn and upon the beer of the red barley.

And let the forms of my father and of my mother be granted to me; the gate-keepers of the stream.

Let room be thrown open for me, let the path be made, and let me sit in any place that I desire.

I am the sharp-horned Bull, who regulateth the sky, the Lord of the risings in heaven; the great Giver of Light, who issueth from Flame;

the Bond of Time, richly supplied with years; the god in Lion form, to whom is given a march of Glory.

I execrate, I execrate, I do not eat that which my Genius execrateth.

Let it not enter into my stomach, let it not approach to my hands, let me not tread upon it with my sandals.

Let me not drink lye, let me not advance headlong in the Netherworld.

I am the possessor of bread in Heliopolis, who hath bread in Heaven with Re, and bread upon earth with Seb.

It is the Sektit boat which hath brought it from the house of the great god in Heliopolis.

I am gladdened in my very entrails, and am associated with the divine mariners, who circle round to the East of Heaven. I eat as they eat, and I feed upon what they feed. I eat bread from the house of the Lord of offerings.

Mummy preserved at Giza.
Below: Sarcophagus.

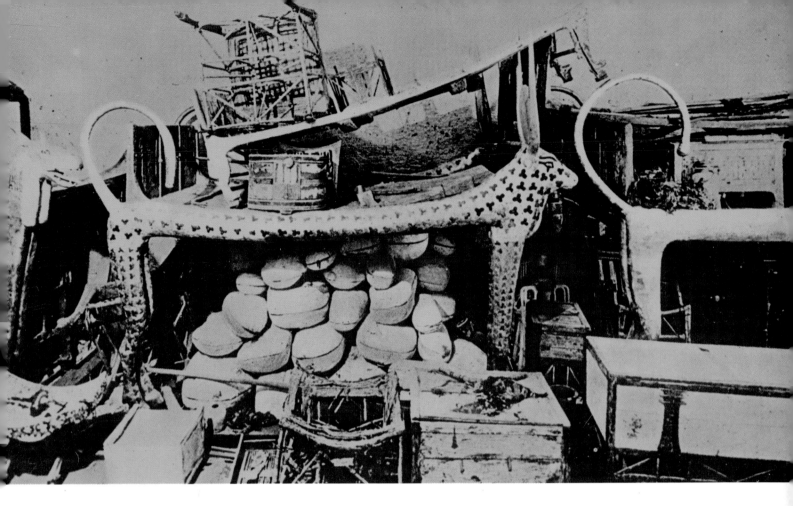

*Photograph of the interior of Tutenkhamen's Tomb at the time of its discovery: furnishings and grave goods for the
Pharaoh (antechamber).*
Below: Funeral boat. Family and friends accompany the deceased to his final resting place.

I execrate, I execrate! I do not eat it.
Dirt is what I execrate; I do not eat it.
I execrate lye, I do not drink it.

Let me not approach it with my fingers, let me not tread upon it with my sandals.

Seb, the father of Osiris, hath ordained that I should not eat dirt or drink lye, but my father hath four times said that I should eat of the red corn.

There are seven loaves in Heaven at Heliopolis with Re, and there are seven loaves upon earth with Seb, and there are seven loaves with Osiris.

The deceased here describes the ideal conditions for eternal bliss: freedom of access to the Underworld, the preservation of a single intact body, complete with its various organs and limbs, and a reliable supply of food and drink. He also evokes the Egyptians' fear of being compelled, in the Underworld, to eat and drink their own waste matter.

Let the two doors of Heaven be opened to me: let the two doors of Earth be opened to me: let the bolts of Seb open to me, and let the First Mansion be opened to me, that he may behold me who hath kept guard over me: and let him unloose me who hath wound his arms around me and hath fastened his arms upon me into the earth.

Let the Re-hunit be opened to me, let me pass into the Re-hunit; let the Re-hunit be given to me, that I may come forth by day whithersoever my heart desireth.

Let me have possession of my heart, let me have possession of my Whole heart; let me have possession of my mouth, let me have possession of my legs, let me have possession of my arms, let me have possession of my limbs absolutely; let me have possession of my funeral meals, let me have possession of air, let me have possession of water, let me have possession of the stream, let me have possession of the river, let me have possession of the banks.

Let me have possession of all things soever which were ritually offered for me in the Netherworld. Let me have possession of the table which was made for me upon earth—the solicitations which were uttered for me "that he may feed upon the bread of Seb."

That which I execrate, I eat it not. Let me

Photograph showing the two lids of a sarcophagus.

Anubis and Thoth weigh the heart of a dead man before Horus. (Painted casket, at the Louvre).

feed upon the bread of the red corn of the Nile in a pure place, let me sip beer of the red corn of the Nile in a pure place; let me sit under the branches of the palm trees in Heliopolis in the train of Hathor, when the solar orb broadeneth, as she proceedeth to Heliopolis with the writings of the divine words of the Book of Thoth.

Let me have possession of my heart, let me have possession of my Whole heart; let me have possession of my arms, let me have possession of my legs, let me have possession of my funeral meals, let me have possession of air, let me have possession of water, let me have possession of the stream, let me have possession of the river, let me have possession of the barks.

Let me have possession of all things soever which were ritually offered for me in the Netherworld. Let me have possession of the table which was made for me upon earth.

Let me be raised up on the left and on the right; let me be raised up on the right and on the left.

This is one of the spells contained in some versions of the Chapters of Transformations. The deceased claims to have become both a swallow and a scorpion; nothing, however, is left to chance, as he also claims to be virtuous and to have secret knowledge.

I am the Swallow. I am the Swallow. I am the Scorpion, the daughter of the Sun. Oh Gods! delicious is the smell of your fire which comes out of the horizon. Oh thou who art in the place! Guardian of the corner, lead me. Give me thy arm. I keep a watch in the Pool of Fire. I come by my efforts. I have come, having the writing. I open; what do I say I have seen? It is Horus steering the bark, giving place to his father. It is Seth, the son of Nu, undoing all he has done. I have examined that which is in the sealed place. I have laid my arm on Osiris. I go by my efforts. I have come speaking. Let me open the writing. I am the reckoning which goes in and the account which goes out of the Gate of the Universal Lord. I am washed on my leg. Oh Great One! I have dissipated my sins. I have destroyed my failings, for I have got rid of the sins which detained me on earth. Oh Door-keepers! I have made roads. It is then I am like you. I have come out of the day. I have walked on my feet, I prevail with my steps. I have known the secret roads in the Gates of the fields of the Aahlu. Let me overthrow my oppressors. On earth my body is embalmed.

This spell is addressed to the four sacred apes who sit around the Pool of Fire through which the deceased passes in order to become purified.

On great Four Apes, seated in front of the boat of the Sun, sending truth to the Universal Lord, judging my deficiency and my abundance, welcoming Gods with the fire of their mouths, giving divine offerings to the Gods, meals to the Spirits, living in truth, fed with truth, without fraud, who abominate wickedness! Extract ye all the evil out of me, obliterate ye my faults, annihilate my sins, guard ye, and give ye me to pass the Pylon to go from the plains. I pass through the secret Pylons of the West. Ye ought to give to me food and bread like the Spirits who are going in and coming out of the plains. Thou mayest go, we pardon all thy faults, we annihilate all thy sins. Thou hast been severed from the world, we dissipate all thy sins. Thou hast severed thyself from earth, thou hast dissipated all the sin which detained thee. Come to the Plains. Thou openest the secret doors of the West. Thou comest forth and goest in as thou wishest, like one of the Spirits hailed daily within the horizon.

As a result of the cult of Osiris, the deceased identified themselves with the great god; in their respective papyri of the Book of the Dead, each dead person is called "Osiris-Ani", "Osiris-Hunefer", "Osiris-Anhai" etc. Here the deceased—"the Osiris"—brags of his ability to crush all his enemies.

Hail, oh thou Sun in his ark shining with his light, gleaming with his gleam! detaining millions at his wish, placed in the face of those who see; the Creator in the midst of his boat, who smiteth the Apophis daily, say for the children of Seb, who smiteth the enemies of Osiris, they are crushed by the boat. Horus smites off their heads to the heaven (as) for the

fowls, their thighs to the earth for wild beasts, to the waters for the fishes. The Osiris crushes all evil Spirits, male or female, whether they go from heaven or earth, come out of the waters or cross from the tips of the stars. Thoth cuts them up, —a stone out of the buildings of those who possess the ark of Osiris [?]. The Sun is that Great God, the greatest of smiters, the most powerful of terrifiers, he washes in your blood, he dips in your gore. For the Osiris crushes them in the boat of his father the Sun. Horus is the Osiris. His mother Isis produced him, Nephthys nursed him, likewise they made the conspirators of Set to turn back for Horus. When they see the crown placed before him they fall down on their faces. Osiris Un-nefer has made his justification against his enemies in heaven, on earth, amongst the chief of the Gods and Goddesses.

Designed and produced by
Productions Liber SA

© Productions Liber SA,
and Editions Minerva SA
Fribourg - Genève, 1979/1984

Printed in Spain